Energy Almanac

Astrological Insights & Holistic Resources For The Year Ahead

Veilleux, Tam | *Energy Almanac, 2021*

BiG SKY

P U B L I S H I N G
fun. fresh. transformational.

Published by Big Sky Publishing, LLC
Edited by Susan Puiia
Design by Kendra Cagle, 5 Lakes Design

ISBN-13 **Perfect Bound:** 9781647751753
ISBN-13 **Spiral Bound :** 9781647751760
ISBN-13 **Hardcover:** 9781647751777

www.shopBigSky.com

Dedication

◇◆◇

Millennials, you are the
Age of Aquarius. Lead us well.

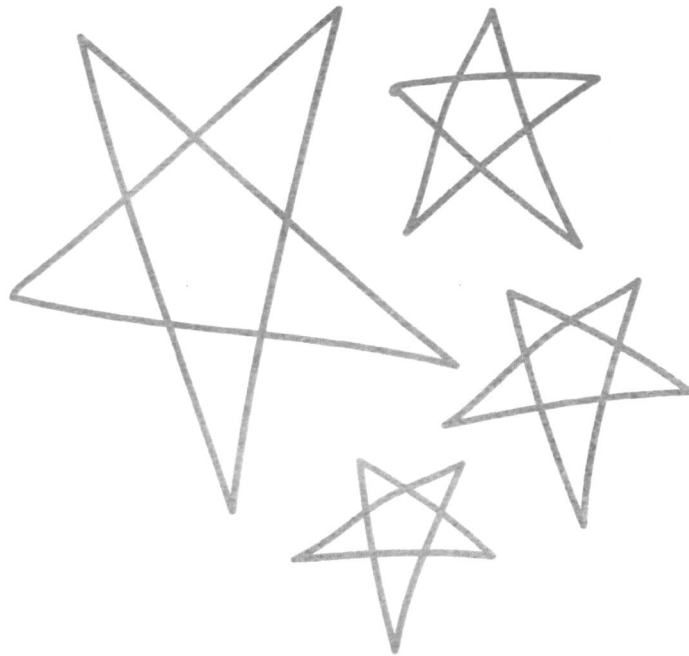

♡ Love the Energy Almanac? Share on social media: #EnergyAlmanac ♡

Page 3

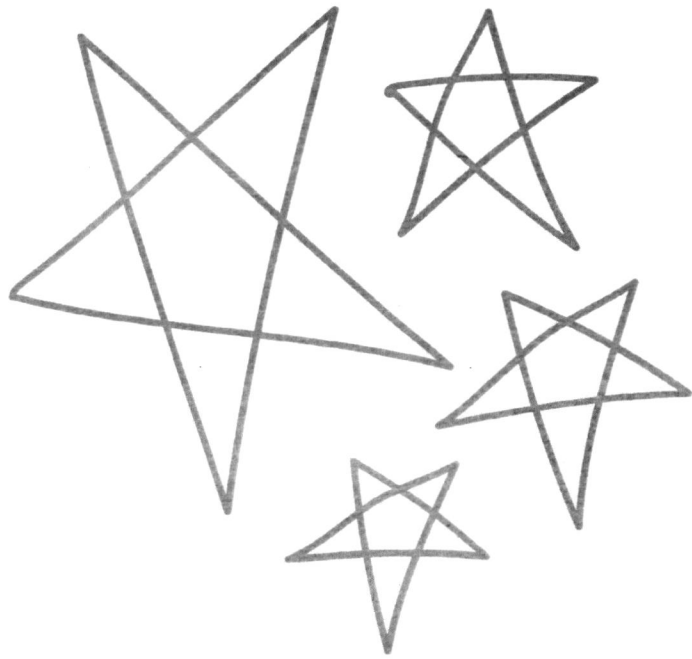

From the Publisher

◇ ◇ ◇

It is from the midst of the 2020 "spiritual quarantine" that The Energy Almanac for 2021 was birthed. With Saturn in Aquarius came the first, in recent memory, need to be squirreled away. With temperatures rising north both physically and emotionally, much of the population found themselves with time on their hands to ponder. What is the meaning of life? Why am I here? What is this about? Why now? As I sat pouring over some of my favorite ancient Sufi poetry, so elegantly translated to English, I happened across one potential answer.

"WHENEVER THEY REBUILD AN OLD BUILDING, THEY MUST FIRST OF ALL DESTROY THE OLD ONE." –RUMI

Ahh, Rumi to the rescue to bring some sense to a nonsensical situation. Life as we know it is changing. The destruction of old beliefs and value systems was at hand, and a quarantine would keep us safe and allow us to re-engage with our spiritual selves. It was a slowing of the machine. The Energy Almanac astrology for 2020 had seen something coming though we couldn't call out the actual form in which it would arrive. Arrive it did, as a worldwide pandemic. And now, as 2021 arrives, it's plain to see that adjustments are still needed.

As you set about your planning for the year ahead, keep in mind the three words that we feel best represents what the astrology will bring:

ADJUST. BALANCE. CO-CREATE.

With this year's Energy Almanac, we welcome many new writers. I hope you will seek them out and share your thoughts with them, follow their social media accounts, and sign up for their newsletters. The work they did while in the thick of the pandemic was nothing short of remarkable. Their contact information and bios are in the back of this Almanac along with their website URLs.

While I was doing some early writing for 2021, I became intensely aware of the need for flexibility and versatility in the year ahead. The image that kept showing itself was a tree. Able to bend and move with the wind without breaking, trees, with their deep roots, are the best example I could think of to demonstrate what our human selves could lean into this year.

"Life is a balance of holding on and letting go," said that wise ancient one, Rumi. 2021 may be the year to fully understand this. Stay strong at your core like the tree's trunk. Be flexible, like the tree limbs, and let go what isn't serving you anymore, like the leaves. The key phrase for 2021 is "Status quo or forward flow."

Lastly, do read the disclaimer here in The Energy Almanac before you take on any of our suggested holistic resources. Your life choices are yours. Your health and well-being, physically, mentally, emotionally, and spiritually are between you and God. Don't take any advice from within the covers of this publication that doesn't ring true for you. Your instincts are strong, honor them.

Please visit our online shop for the holistic resources you need to round out and bring balance and flexibility to your 2021. Go to: **www.shopBigSky.com**

TAM VEILLEUX
Teacher. Healer. Artist. Publisher.

♡ Love the Energy Almanac? Share on social media: #EnergyAlmanac ♡

Page 5

2021 Moon Dates

◇◈◇

NEW MOON	FULL MOON
January 13 in Capricorn	January 28 in Leo
February 11 in Aquarius	February 27 in Virgo
March 13 in Pisces	March 28 in Libra
April 11 in Aries	April 26 in Scorpio
May 11 in Taurus	May 26 in Sagittarius
June 10 in Gemini	June 24 in Capricorn
July 9 in Cancer	July 23 in Aquarius
August 8 in Leo	August 22 in Aquarius
September 6 in Virgo	September 20 in Pisces
October 6 in Libra	October 20 in Aries
November 4 in Scorpio	November 19 in Taurus
December 4 in Sagittarius	December 18 in Gemini

Energy Almanac 2021 Edition

How to use the Energy Almanac

Around since the second millennium and used by some of the ancient world's greatest thinkers like Aratus, Ptolemy, Thomas Aquinas, and Roger Bacon, humans have long been able to see the relationship between events on earth and the corresponding location of specific planets. What's to stop modern man and woman from using the heavens as a way of predicting life events? Answer: nothing.

For some solid answers to life's most perplexing questions, we need only look to names, numbers, and astrology.

Planets are energetic balls of light radiating consciousness and archetypal information. We are energetic beings with consciousness. When the energy of the archetype is in our orb of influence, we innately feel it and act accordingly. Knowing the personality of each planet, the attire it might don (zodiac signs), and which life area it is sitting in helps you to write your plan from a more powerful perspective.

To this writer, astrology can be both predictive and reflective.

In your journal you can look back to the astrology that was at play during any episode and connect the dots to those events. Looking ahead, it's easy to see what's coming and how to address the topic with grace.

Taking a good look at how the planets are positioned and what the meaning is behind that position offers you amazing insight to what you can expect to play out. When playing a game, there's an advantage to having a strategy. In the 2021 edition of The Energy Almanac our goal is to help you in the game of life.

The Energy Almanac as a regular reference can help you in making decisions. We will share insights about global movements you might experience in the months ahead. This Latin proverb "Forewarned is forearmed" is powerful, and isn't that the truth? We suggest three steps for using the 2021 Energy Almanac.

First, as you move through the 12 months making up 2021, it is recommended that you give this publication regular readings. Read through once for a solid overview of what's happening for the year. Highlight the pieces of information that intrigue you. Create a list of relative dates and happenings before giving the book a second reading. This time seek data that will affect your personal or professional decision making by again underlining pertinent pieces. Add any dates and information from these initial reads into your personal calendaring system for the year.

Second, read the Almanac monthly and weekly. Start each month by pulling out the art and framing it. It's a reflection tool meant to be seen and referenced weekly. Become cognizant of which aspects and transits are highlighted each week and how you might need to traverse them relative to your own game of life. Place the Energy Almanac itself in a conspicuous location where you will bump into it regularly. Pick one day each week to interact with this information.

Last, break your mother's rule. Write in this book. If you know you have travel to do, decisions to make, health issues to face, jot these things down, weekly or monthly, and reread the printed insights. Let the information guide you. As the days and weeks pass, write the results of your week. If you happened to find yourself being super analytical for a range of time, add that in the Almanac next to the information about the planets at play during that time period. You will begin to connect the dots about your own personal relationship to that planet. Remember to capture the more global goings on too. Pay attention to politics, education, medicine, weather. It's all impacted by the movements of the planets.

Use the holistic resources as suggested by our hand-picked experts in their field.

This year you have numerology, gemstones, essential oils, Hatha yoga, nutrition, and supplementation. Your journaling question is ready for you too.

You are invited to play the game of life at a whole new level; connect the dots and see what may be ahead for you. But remember, as evolutionary astrologer Stephen Forrest says, "Every front has a back." Keep a close eye on the planets, and both their positive and negative aspects. This will give you hints to possibilities that might arise in your inner or outer world. The planets have a plan for you and The Energy Almanac reveals them all. Plan accordingly.

How the Planets Play

PLANETS

Recall if you will the Roman myths we learned. Think of the ten planets as actors from those tales. Each planet is named after a character in a story with its own personality and traits. Planets tell us what is being worked on. For example, in mythology Saturn was the god of time and taught agriculture to his people. Saturn rules time, karma, discipline and responsibility.

ZODIAC SIGNS

The twelve zodiac signs can be thought of as pieces of clothing that the planets might wear for a period of time. Each sign has specific qualities, traits, strengths, weaknesses, and general attitudes toward life. When a planet is traversing in any specific sign, its own personality will be affected by the qualities of the sign. The zodiac sign indicates why and how we might handle life. Example: The zodiac sign of Virgo is known for being analytical, health oriented, mentally astute, detailed, preachy, overwhelmed, self-critical, and uptight.

ASTROLOGICAL HOUSES

The twelve houses of astrology represent where the character of the story will be. It's the stage or scene they will act in. The houses range from internal areas such as values, wishes and goals, shadow work, or identity to more external and tangible areas such as children, money, religion, and career. As a planet moves through a house, that area of life will feel the pressure of said planet.

ASPECTS

Aspects are the specific position the planets have in relation to other planets. There are a dozen or more different planetary line-up potentials, but we've listed the more commonly referenced aspects here.

CONJUNCTION: Harmonious, blended.

OPPOSITION: Disharmonious, dynamic, energizing.

SQUARE: Disharmonious, blocked.

TRINE: Harmonious, energies working together.

SEXTILE: Mostly harmonious (depending on the course of planets involved).

♡   Love the Energy Almanac? Share on social media: #EnergyAlmanac   ♡

Page 9

Planets

Think of the ten planets as actors from the stories of Roman mythology. Each planet is named after a character in a story, each with its own personality and traits.

SUN
describes a general tone of being which colors everything else. It rules Leo.

MOON
represents our feelings and emotions, the receptivity, intuition, imagination and basic feeling tone of a person. It also affects our sense of rhythm and time. It rules Cancer.

MERCURY
is reason, common sense, and that which is rational. It stands for communication; that which is versatile, logical, and dynamic; order, weighing, and evaluating; and the process of learning and skills. It rules Gemini and Virgo.

VENUS
gives us a sense of beauty, the enjoyment of pleasure, aesthetic awareness, love of harmony, sociability, and taking pleasure in relationships and eroticism. It rules Libra and Taurus.

MARS
represents the energy and drive of a person, their courage, determination, the freedom of spontaneous impulse. It also describes the readiness for action, the way one goes about doing things, as well as simple aggression. It rules Aries.

JUPITER
represents the search for individual meaning and purpose, optimism, hope, and a sense of justice, along with faith, a basic philosophy of life, wealth, religion, spiritual growth, and expansion. It rules Sagittarius.

SATURN
shows how we experience "reality", where we meet with resistance and discover our limitations. It represents the conscience, moral convictions, and structure. It also tells us about our powers of endurance and the ability to concentrate. It lends qualities like earnestness, caution, and reserve. It rules Capricorn.

URANUS
stands for intuition and represents originality, independence, and an openness for all that is new, unknown, and unusual. A sort of wrong-headed contrariness is also associated with this planet. It rules Aquarius.

NEPTUNE
gives us the mysterious and supersensory, opens doors to mystical experience, and to the creative, intuitive, and imaginative. Watch for deception, illusion, and false appearances. Neptune is associated with drug use and all kinds of pseudo-realities. It rules Pisces.

PLUTO
describes how we deal with personal and non-personal power. It is how we meet the demonic and magical. Pluto addresses our regenerative powers, and our capacity for radical change and rebirth; it is passionate, intense, and global. It rules Scorpio.

Zodiac Signs

—◇◇◇—

Each zodiac sign carries specific tendencies and traits. The planets are influenced by these qualities as they pass through the sign.

ARIES

MARCH 21-APRIL 19

Fire. Ruled by Mars. Brave, Direct, Fearless, Bold, Independent, Natural born leaders. Aggressive, Pushy, Selfish, Inconsistent.

TAURUS

APRIL 20-MAY 20

Earth. Ruled by Venus. Steady, Loyal, Tenacious, Trustworthy, Patient. Resistant to change, Stubborn, Materialistic, Indulgent

GEMINI

MAY 21-JUNE 20

Air. Ruled by Mercury. Intelligent, Adaptable, Communicative, Agile, Socially connected. Talkative, Superficial, Cunning, Exaggerating.

CANCER

JUNE 21-JULY 22

Water. Ruled by the Moon. Nurturing, Supportive, Compassionate, Loving, Healing. Dependent, Indirect, Moody, Passive-aggressive, Holds on too long.

LEO

JULY 23-AUGUST 22

Fire. Ruled by the Sun. Brave, Generous, Charismatic, Fun, Playful, Warm, Protective. Egotistical, Controlling, Drama King/Queen, Dominating, Shows off.

VIRGO

AUGUST 23-SEPTEMBER 22

Earth. Ruled by Mercury. Modest, Orderly, Practical, Down to earth, Logical, Altruistic, Organized. Obsessive, Perfectionist, Critical, Overly analytical.

LIBRA

SEPTEMBER 23-OCTOBER 22

Air. Ruled by Venus. Charming, Diplomatic, Polished, Sweet natured, Social. Indecisive, Superficial, Out of balance, Gullible, People pleasing.

SCORPIO

OCTOBER 23-NOVEMBER 21

Water. Ruled by Mars & Pluto. Passionate, Driven, Perceptive, Determined, Sacrificing, Emotional Depth. Vindictive, Jealous, Paranoid, Destructive, Possessive, Passive-aggressive.

SAGITTARIUS

NOVEMBER 22-DECEMBER 21

Fire. Ruled by Jupiter. Ambitious, Lucky, Optimistic, Enthusiastic, Open-minded, Moral. Restless, Blunt, Irresponsible, Tactless, Lazy, Overly indulgent.

CAPRICORN

DECEMBER 22-JANUARY 19

Earth. Ruled by Saturn. Driven, Disciplined, Responsible, Persistent, Business minded. Pessimistic, Greedy, Cynical, Rigid, Miserly, Ruthless.

AQUARIUS

JANUARY 20-FEBRUARY 18

Air. Ruled by Saturn & Uranus. Intelligent, Inventive, Humanitarian, Friendly, Reformative. Emotionally detached, Impersonal, Scattered, Non-committal.

PISCES

FEBRUARY 19-MARCH 20

Water. Ruled by Neptune. Mystical, Intuitive, Compassionate, Romantic, Creative, Sensitive. Escapist, Victims, Codependent, Unrealistic, Submissive, Dependent.

Energy Almanac 2021 Edition

Planning According to the Light Cycles

From the publisher. *In our desire to make a more robust product, the 2021 edition of the Energy Almanac includes information you can use to guide the pace of your projects and goals. This year's astrologer, Shellie Enteen, carefully explains the applicable cycles of light. In each of the weekly articles of The Energy Almanac, you will find icons representing the quarterly cycle you are in. Relate the icon to the kind of work to do during the current time period. The flow that is accessible when working with the cycles is freeing. Enjoy!*

All things in life have cycles. Like our own breath, they exhibit a clear beginning, waxing, peak point of transition before a waning cycle, and an ending. So it is with the "lights" in astronomy called the Sun and Moon. With both Sun and Moon, a waxing cycle is good for growth, the point of greatest light marks fruition and the waning of light is a time for sharing and readjusting. The time of least light is for releasing.

Knowing the meanings of the cycles helps us choose the right one for our needs.

The Solar Cycles are noted by the four quarters also known as a solstice or equinox. The Solar Cycle begins with the winter solstice when the light hours will begin to grow. Each quarter is divided into two cycles of emphasis, called cross quarters. For purposes of The Energy Almanac four quarters are referenced, each with two cycles.

A NOTE ABOUT ECLIPSES:

Each year, at least two of the New and Full Moons are also a Solar or Lunar Eclipse. These take place when the sun, earth, and moon align so that the new moon will cover the face of the sun from the earth's perspective (the solar eclipse) or the earth will block the sun's light from reaching the full moon (the lunar eclipse).

An eclipse indicates a major change will arrive. It has a six-month influence and can be felt as far as six weeks before it occurs. The Solar Eclipse is about identity and marks a change in an outer world circumstance; the Lunar Eclipse is about feelings and marks a change in relationships. Avoid beginning new ventures on or during the week before and after an eclipse.

THE LUNAR NODES:

NORTH NODE

The two Lunar Nodes are a specific moving point in space where the Sun and Moon's orbital paths around the earth intersect. One node represents north, the other represents the south. Unlike the planets, the moon's nodes move in a clockwise direction (i.e. Taurus toward Aries) around the zodiac. The North Node much like Jupiter, is a point where benefits are found. It represents a positive evolutionary direction, what we need to learn, and our mission. The South Node is considered as Saturn, a point of constriction. It represents old instincts that must be transformed.

SOUTH NODE

Energy Almanac 2021 Edition

FOUR QUARTERS OF SOLAR CYCLES
(in the Northern Hemisphere)

FIRST QUARTER
Keywords:
Visioning/Planting

At this time, there is an increase in the hours of light. It's a time of beginnings, perfect for visioning new ideas about your life direction. As longer days become more apparent and new growth appears in nature, we discover the areas of life where we should plant seeds for the success of our goals. Things are now set in motion.

SECOND QUARTER
Keywords:
Nurturing/Acquiring

This is a time of more light which is accompanied by more greening upon the earth and more general energy. Make time for nourishing activities and seek contacts that support your goals and interests. Gather your success tools and use them to nurture your goals. Visualize the manifestation of your goals.

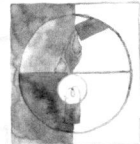

THIRD QUARTER
Keywords:
Celebrate/Share

This quarter begins with the time of greatest light. Celebrate the fruition of your work and honor the resources that have supported your goals. Notice what is yet to be achieved or what should be released. Share the gifts of your harvest and knowledge and make note of what worked or didn't work and why.

FOURTH QUARTER
Keywords: Organize, Realign/Release

There are now more hours of darkness. The last harvests arrive. Celebrate, organize, and preserve. Settle debts and explore the balance of giving and receiving. As winter begins, life grows below the earth. Apply this to your own life by turning inward to reflect. Recognize and release things that no longer represent the authentic you.

FOUR QUARTERS OF LUNAR CYCLES

FIRST QUARTER
New Moon to waxing Half Moon.
Visioning/Planting

The first quarter is time for visioning and planting the seeds of our goals.

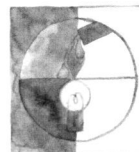

SECOND QUARTER
Waxing Half Moon to the Full Moon.
Nurture/Acquire

The second quarter is for taking action, nourishing, and gathering all necessary information and tools for success.

THIRD QUARTER
Full Moon to the waning Half Moon.
Celebrate/Share

The harvest of the full moon ends this second quarter and begins the third quarter. This is also called the disseminating phase. It's time to share what we've gained or learned from the harvest.

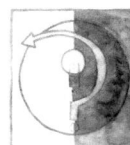

FOURTH QUARTER
Waning Half Moon to the New Moon.
Realign/Release

Assess your results to see where improvement can be made. This is a good time to see what changes can be made to increase future harvests.

♡ Love the Energy Almanac? Share on social media: #EnergyAlmanac ♡

Energy Almanac 2021 Edition

Page 13

From Our Contributors

—◇◆◇—

ASTROLOGY PERSPECTIVES FOR 2021

by Shellie Enteen, Astrologer

The energy flow of 2021 represents an adjustment in recognizing the power of our personal energy and its application toward a positive outcome. The new year will find you constantly battling attempts to put structures and systems in place because of a constant stream of surprising changes in finances. Personal values will be under constant scrutiny as well.

Consciousness is expanding rapidly. It's best we let go of comfortable beliefs to take in new concepts. Other lessons in 2021 come through thinking and communicating in harmonious ways to allow others to express their own ideas.

In the first year of a new 20-year cycle with Aquarian influence, the focus is on freedom and responsible concern for the larger group. We may find ourselves wondering how far electronic technology will expand and how that may affect personal connections and relationships. How will social media manage this?

In the year ahead, we are learning to navigate cultural shifts for the Aquarian age. Will there be a new focus on freedom, safe sources of energy, and a humanitarian desire for the good of the whole? Or will greater restraints on individuality be applied while more technology takes over jobs and human interaction? As we move through this time of uncertainty, create a vision of what you'd like to see and empower this vision with your thoughts and actions.

MAJOR TRANSITS IN 2021:

- **South node in Sagittarius** means our evolutionary direction remains focused on giving up old beliefs and rigid perceptions.
- **North node in Gemini** shows us the way forward which is through expanding knowledge and improving communication.
- **Mars travels from late Aries to mid-Sagittarius.** Where Mars transits, we can expect plenty of take-action energy and movement.
- **Jupiter in Aquarius** will take the expansion of consciousness to new realms.
- **Saturn is firmly in Aquarius this year,** bringing lessons in freedom, equality, and a need for detached objectivity in the areas of goal setting, friendship, and group affiliation. An air sign, Aquarius deals with the unseen realms. Whether applied to thought, sound, electronics, or our life force energy, it's time to upgrade how we experience, receive, and use energy. Aquarius also rules electricity and electronic tools, like computers and cell phones, and also information received through unseen energies, like astrology. This is a potent transit bringing fundamental changes.
- **Saturn in Aquarius has a big impact on 2021 with three squares to Uranus in Taurus.** This transit represents the tension that occurs when obstacles (Saturn) are in the way of change (Uranus). Some people or institutions may be holding onto the status quo, even when they would be better served by shifting. It's time perhaps to learn the wisdom of both ancient and new ways. As these squares approach, in personal and outer life, it may feel like two stones are rubbing against each other until they create sparks. The exact squares to Uranus in Taurus take place on February 17th, June 14th, and December 24th. Watch for tension.
- **Neptune in Pisces moves toward a sextile to Pluto in Capricorn,** infusing 2021 with a welcome combination of creativity and transformation, spiritual awareness, and worldly manifestation.

At the start of a new 20-year era, you succeed by seeking inner guidance and through staying open to refining how you operate and when you operate. Methods and timelines are shifting. Allow for and adjust to changes by grounding your personal energy. If you check your progress and make any necessary adjustments along the way, 2021 becomes a year to advance goals and see results.

THE NUMEROLOGY OF 2021

by Dara Bailey, Numerologist and Spiritual Advisor

Freedom is necessary for you to ride the high vibrational influence of the 5 year of 2021. 2 + 0 + 2 + 1 = 5

Change is a natural part of life, and this year will demonstrate that. This is your year to implement modifications in your life which will carry you to your most desired destination. 2021 is radiating a constant vibrational frequency of change, flexibility, and freedom. Mental dexterity is key should you choose to fully be with the energy of 2021. Variety in who you surround yourself with could supply answers.

There may be a turning point for you this year. Just look at the natural design of the five. Movement and pivots all indicate a year where we will be on our toes. Using gratitude, mindfulness, meditation, and submission, you will gracefully create an incredible life. Embrace all the new adventures. They are all reflections of a life you've created.

For each month of 2021 I have taken the number of the month and added it to 5, the number representing this year. Example: January (1) + 2021 (5). January is a 6 month in a 5 year. Both numerical influences will be active.

FOR THE LOVE OF GEMSTONES

by Kate Sarton Dunn, Gem Enthusiast and Coach

Because you are reading the Energy Almanac, you probably already acknowledge, to some degree, the presence of energy in the universe and in your life. It will be no surprise that this carries over into the natural world, and specifically, stones. Stones have aspects (dare I say personalities?) as unique as each human being. The eye-catching beauty of stones and the effects of their energy on the world around them have fascinated humans for thousands of years.

Gemstones are very easy to play with. Simply being in their presence is all it takes. What could you create in your life by playing with these energies? As you engage with and receive from beautiful stones, stop to notice if anything feels different. Do you notice anything in your body? Does your focus shift? Does your mind clear? Do you find yourself drawn to certain colors or aspects? You don't have to be an expert to have your own knowing and awareness. Stones are one more way to cultivate your intuition and knowing. The stones offered in this book are by no means an exhaustive list; they are a spark and a place where you might begin. Are you ready?

WAYS TO USE STONES:

- Wear stone(s) daily to immerse yourself in the energies. Keep one in your pocket or wear a bracelet or piece of jewelry with the suggested stones.
- Use for meditation and breathwork. Hold the stone in your hand or let it rest on the chakra/s it corresponds to.
- Use a set of gemstone meditation beads with the suggested mantras for each month.
- Speak your goals and targets aloud while holding a stone. It is great for actualizing your manifestations.
- Use stones to aid your sleep. Keep stone under your pillow, on your bedside table, or hanging over your bed.
- Keep stones where you spend a good portion of your day: at your office, on your desk, the living room, the kitchen, your car, or your bedroom.

Energy Almanac 2021 Edition

♡ Love the Energy Almanac? Share on social media: #EnergyAlmanac ♡

Page 15

ESSENTIAL OILS

by Meegan Sciretto, Health Coach

Essential oils have been prized for their therapeutic and aromatic powers for thousands of years. They offer incredible benefits for vitality, energy, clarity, calm, and spiritual upliftment. Pure essential oils offer natural choices for personal care, family wellness, home cleaning, body care products, and more.

When choosing essential oils, it is important to select 100% pure therapeutic grade oils that have been rigorously tested by independent labs to ensure purity and potency. Select companies that use plants grown indigenously and sourced ethically and sustainably. This supports local farmers across the globe.

Essential oils have become quite popular over the past few years. It is important to remember that they are potent and should be used safely and with care. If you are new to essential oils and uncertain about proper use, please read the safety article in the resource section of this publication and do consult an aromatherapist, essential oil educator, or an essential oil reference guide.

SAFE ESSENTIAL OIL USE

Purchase quality organic, pesticide free, or wild harvested essential oils that have undergone third party GC/MS (Gas Chromatography/Mass Spectrometry) testing from companies who share these results. This information can be found on the oil company's website or printed materials.

Know your oil. Make sure each bottle of essential oil lists most, if not all, of these categories: the Latin name, method of extraction, cultivation, plant part used, country of origin, and distillation date.

Think sustainably. Did you know it takes 30-50 roses to distill one drop of Rose Otto essential oil? That's a lot of plant material for one tiny drop. Buy and use only what you need, reducing consumer waste and protecting the environment for future generations.

Yes, always dilute your essential oils in a carrier before use. A carrier is a liquid or semi-solid (usually vegetable-derived) base such as Jojoba, Apricot, Olive, Grapeseed, Coconut, and even Cocoa Butter. If you're not sure how to dilute oils, see below.

1. **Find your Standard Dilution Rate below for the individual receiving application.**
   - *2 - 6 years old use 1 % dilution*
   - *6 - 15 years old use 2 % dilution*
   - *15 + years old use 3 % dilution*
   - *Use 1 % or less for full body application, daily, or long term use.*
   - *You can use up to 10% dilution for small areas or acute situations.*
2. **Establish how much base/carrier you need.** Are you making a roll on for spot application or are you making a full body massage oil?
3. **Use the dilution chart on the next page** to find out how many drops of essential oils you need to safely and effectively create an appropriate dilution.

Volume of base	0.5%	1%	2%	3%	4%	5%	10%
15 ml (½ oz)	2	4	9	13	18	22	44
30 ml (1 oz)	4	9	18	27	36	45	90

Keep essential oils away from eyes, ears, and mucous membranes, as most essential oils have the potential to be mucous membrane and skin irritants, especially if they are old or oxidized.

Consult with a certified aromatherapist and/or your healthcare practitioner to evaluate the appropriate selection of an oil, dilution rate, method of use, duration of use, potential drug interactions, or contraindications before using essential oils for the following:

- For internal use. Essential Oils are highly concentrated botanicals that deserve safe care and handling and have potential for adverse reactions.
- If pregnant, breastfeeding, or under the age of three.
- If severely ill, elderly, undergoing surgery, taking multiple medications, or diagnosed with hypertension or epilepsy.

To learn more about safe and effective essential oil use through maternity, motherhood, and for women's health, contact Stephanie Veilleux-Welch: Certified Aromatherapist & Childbirth Doula at **www.LavendoulaME.com.**

LIFE WITH YOGA
by Kelly Smith Cassidy, Yoga Teacher, Artist, and Astrologer

Many students of yoga practice for many years and still find new meaning in even the simplest of poses. One may feel like they have mastered yoga, only to discover a new subtlety that they had never noticed before, bringing new depth to their practice. Others may have practiced the physical yoga asana practice and feel that something is still missing. They may then explore yoga philosophies to complement their yoga practice.

Wherever you are in your practice, or even if you have never practiced yoga at all, the yoga sections of this almanac will provide insights, spark new understanding about this ancient practice, and invite the yogic philosophy into your life.

Use these monthly yoga insights to go deeper in your yoga practice or discover new methods and techniques that you may want to explore more on your own.

♡ Love the Energy Almanac? Share on social media: #EnergyAlmanac ♡

Page 17

CHEW ON THIS
by Melissa Rivera, Health Coach

Health is wealth. This is why it is so important to really tune in and listen to how food feels in your body. Start noticing the way what you eat affects your mood, your energy, and your sleep. The tips in The Energy Almanac are intended to encourage you to look at food in a different way. Start the year off mindfully and set the tone. Food is medicine and our gut is the gateway to disease. Remember, meaning what feels good in your body may not feel good in your partner's or children's.

The suggestions in this almanac are guidelines only. Learn what works for you and don't be afraid to try something new! Add diversity to your diet to ensure you are delivering a mixture of all the vitamins, minerals and nutrients your body needs for vibrance. Healthy eating is a lifestyle, not a quick-fix. Trust that small dietary changes over time add up to long-term success towards making eating healthy part of your daily routine. Most important, have fun with food and share it often with those you love.

HEALTHY YOU
by Raymond Veilleux, The Health Medium

As you lean into a more natural way of addressing your health, you may come to realize the many aspects of your physical self. We really are mind, body, and spirit. The energy we emit as human beings can be amplified through simple techniques that are shared in these pages. If you're feeling low, the Four Thumps may be just the quick fix you need to boost your energy, while drinking enough water will change how your body functions. And general supplementation will always help you to feel more complete because your body will respond to the right fuel.

From my years as a health intuitive, I've learned that we come in many shapes, sizes, and attitudes. My intuitive guidance has very rarely steered me wrong, but always, always check in with your own intuition before taking on any health advice, and do read the disclaimer in the front of this book. Know that your health is between you and God.

BOOK BONUSES

It's with great enthusiasm that the collaborators of The Energy Almanac created incredible extras for you to play with. Go to this URL to sign up for audios, cheat sheets, and other special offers.

www.choosebigchange.com/bonus21

THE AGE OF AQUARIUS

= FOR THE COMMON GOOD OF ALL INVOLVED.

♄ SATURN

SENSIBILITY
LESSONS
TIMING

♃ JUPITER

EXPANSION
HOPE
ABUNDANCE

2021

EXPECT AN UPGRADE TO HOW YOU EXPERIENCE ENERGY.

innovation

HIGH TECH TIMES

collaboration & COMMUNITY

consciousness & INTUITION

freedom

TOOLS: FOR THE AGES

ASK: WHAT WOULD AN INNOVATIVE OUTCOME LOOK LIKE?

USE: QUANTUM THINKING
DETACHED OBSERVATION

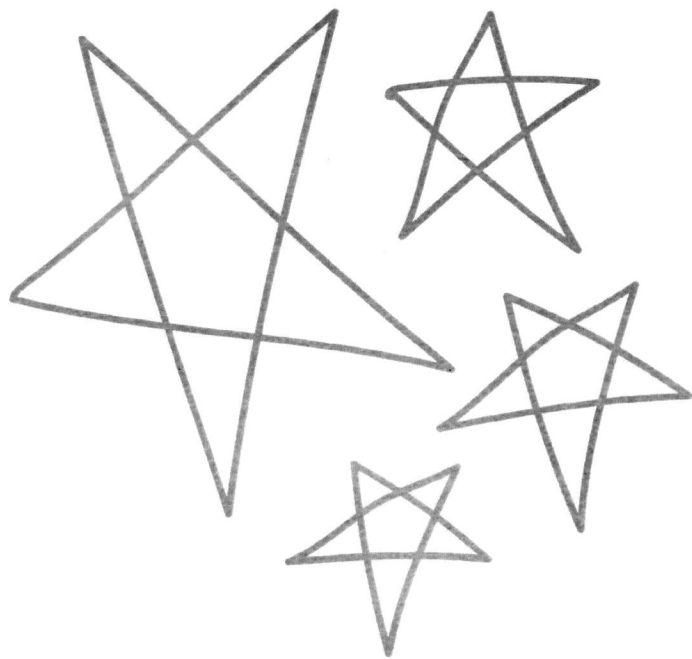

January

OBSERVATION, CAUTION, RESILIENCE

DECEMBER 28, 2020–JANUARY 3, 2021

Do tune in for intuitive guidance concerning timing.
Do not act impulsively.

JANUARY 4–10

Do use your skills of persuasion and diplomacy.
Do not fall prey to discouragement.

JANUARY 11–17

Do keep calm and carry on; this too shall pass.
Do not engage in the struggle.

JANUARY 18–24

Do lean on your spiritual tools.
Do not push or be reactive.

JANUARY 25–31

Do stay focused.
Do not create negative projections.

Don't
MAKE YOURSELF
MISERABLE
WITH WHAT IS
TO COME

OR NOT
TO COME.

WHAT WOULD IT BE LIKE IF I RECEIVED EVERYTHING AND JUDGED NOTHING?

JANUARY 13

NEW MOON IN 23° CAPRICORN
Structures and Responsibility

JANUARY 28

FULL MOON IN 9° LEO
Balance Head and Heart

Energy Almanac 2021 EDITION

♡ Love the Energy Almanac? Share on social media: #EnergyAlmanac ♡

Page 21

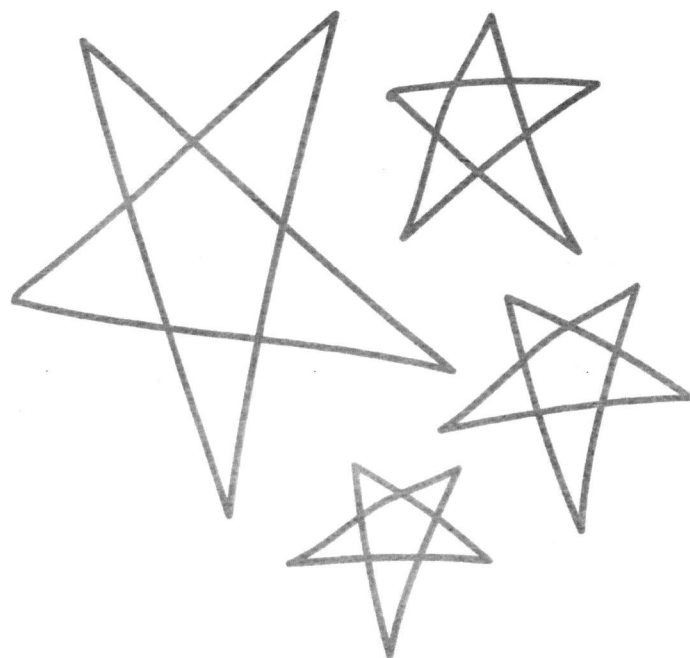

January

——— ◇◈◇ ———

Solar Cycle:
1ST QUARTER
Keywords:
OBSERVATION, CAUTION, RESILIENCE

The last week of December 2020 held the Jupiter Saturn conjunction in Aquarius, heralding a new direction in the collective focus of the world. We now begin to look at the future, your relationships with larger groups and friendships, and how energy can be used in both positive and negative ways. Technology will expand and bring inventions and better ways for communication and connection, but it's best you have structures in place that ensure methods are supportive for the long term.

We begin January filled with momentum for new beginnings and all planets in direct motion. However, four planets in Earth signs indicate an attitude of caution as we explore a new collective emphasis on freedom, equality, and the good of humanity. Earth signs find it hard to shift into new ways and may try to control the Aquarian energy to maintain the status quo. A taste of what this conflict looks like comes when Jupiter in Aquarius squares Uranus in Taurus this month.

There's just no way to sugarcoat the planetary energy coming in mid-January. Aspects from Mercury, Mars, and Jupiter in Aquarius at the same time Uranus is in Taurus bring a particularly unsettled and potentially volatile period from the 11th to 23rd. Surprise, change, anger, and frustration could provoke unwise, potentially harmful actions. The best course is to breathe into emotional reactions, refuse to argue, and find a better time to launch something new. Reawakened optimism comes late in the month.

DATES TO WATCH:

- **January 4-5 Mercury conjunct Pluto.** Notice intense thoughts, obsession, and strict adherence to the letter of the law.

- **January 9-10 Sun sextiles Neptune, Mercury squares Mars, Venus trines Mars, Mercury squares Saturn.** Idealism and positive, productive values are uncomfortably mixed with conflicts in ideas.

- **January 11-12 Mercury conjunct Jupiter, Mars square Saturn, Mercury square Uranus.** Good news and optimism are followed by frustration.

- **January 13 New Moon in Capricorn, Venus trine Uranus, Mars square Saturn.** Positive financial changes meet obstacles that block cooperation. *See January Moons section.*

- **January 14 Sun conjunct Pluto, Venus trine Uranus, Mars square Saturn, Jupiter square Uranus.** The conflict between conservative ideas and forward thinking intensifies.

- **January 15 Sun conjunct Pluto, Mars square Saturn, Jupiter square Uranus.** Helpful attempts to mediate have ended and the conflict continues.

- **January 16-18 Mars square Saturn, Jupiter square Uranus.** It comes down to a conflict between awareness of group needs and the passion to maintain personal and financial resources.

- **January 19-22 Jupiter square Uranus, Mars conjunct Uranus, Mars square Jupiter.** The energies are ripe for sudden, potentially violent actions and changes that upset everyone involved.

- **Jan 23-24 Sun conjunct Saturn, Venus sextile Neptune, Mars square Jupiter.** Tensions begin to ease as a judgment is made and positive ideals reappear. A need for negotiation continues.

- **Jan 26-27 Sun square Uranus, Mars square Jupiter.** Those with authority may not be open to negotiations.

- **Jan 28-29 Leo Full Moon, Sun conjunct Jupiter, Venus conjunct Pluto.** Feelings peak as celebration occurs, benefits arrive, and personal and business partnerships deepen. *See January Moons section.*

- **Jan 30-31 Mercury retrogrades in Aquarius.** Time to review and hold off on the new.

♡ Suns, Moons, and Success. Learn more: www.ChooseBigChange.com ♡

Energy Almanac 2021 EDITION

Page 23

JANUARY ASTROLOGY BY THE WEEKS

DECEMBER 28, 2020 – JANUARY 3, 2021	**Lunar Signs:** GEMINI, CANCER, LEO, VIRGO **Lunar Cycle:** 2ND QUARTER, 3RD QUARTER

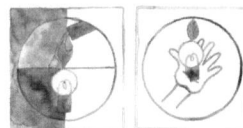

A new 20-year era of cultural focus began at December 2020's Winter Solstice with the Jupiter Saturn conjunction in Aquarius. A Cancer Full Moon reminded us of the need to balance home, security issues, and nurturing with public life and career as 2021 begins. Mercury sextile Neptune softens your approach to public life.

A sense of optimism and new beginnings fills this week. However, a conservative approach is suggested and supported by five planets in earth signs as January begins. Don't be surprised if the strong desire you have to get things moving is stifled.

Late in the week, notice an intuitive understanding of how to and when you might approach those in authority who may hold a piece of the puzzle you need.

Shadow:
We have the urge to take risks and act on our goals, but we have a way to go before we can see how the Jupiter Saturn conjunction will play out in our lives and in the world. Hold off on taking action.

JANUARY 4-10	**Lunar Signs:** VIRGO, LIBRA, SCORPIO, SAGITTARIUS **Lunar Cycle:** 3RD QUARTER, 4TH QUARTER

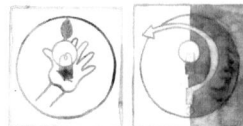

Mercury conjunct Pluto is about obsessive thinking. Neptune squares the nodes and Mars enters Taurus; intuition chooses and passions could shift. Mercury enters Capricorn, Venus enters Aquarius, and Sun sextiles Neptune, all indicating a shift for thinking, and love can be combined with positive visions. Mercury square Mars, Venus trine Mars shows love works better than reason. Mercury joins Saturn for serious thought. Mars in Taurus brings passion to personal finance, while Venus in Capricorn values success, and Mercury in Aquarius thinks about the future. PHEW!

Goals that seem important are scheduled to undergo changes when thinking, motivation, and values shift this week. If you try to apply reason, you'll be stuck on a seesaw of ideas.

Tune in for guidance to resolve a challenge between opposing points of view. Discord due to strong, stubborn differences between thoughts and desires makes Saturday a time to avoid discussion. Use the tender art of persuasion instead. An alliance of practicality and drive to acquire can be formed both internally and externally.

Romantic energy is strong on Saturday evening while Sunday could bring bad news and/or a serious, gloomy turn of mind. Realistic expectations and considered decisions are the plus side, but don't give in to fears or discouragement.

Shadow:
Thoughts on the future, head in the clouds, you may stumble over things that you could have avoided. Or maybe you missed the detour sign? Work on being present.

JANUARY 11-17

Lunar Signs:
SAGITTARIUS, CAPRICORN, AQUARIUS, PISCES
Lunar Cycle:
4TH QUARTER, 1ST QUARTER

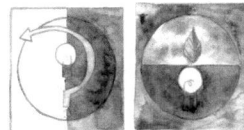

Mercury conjunct Jupiter, Mercury square Uranus indicates that your optimism requires reevaluation. Capricorn New Moon, Mars square Saturn could mean that your goal setting may be accompanied by frustration. Venus trine Uranus, Sun conjunct Pluto indicates practical help combined with strong leadership. Jupiter square Uranus is the expansion of consciousness that struggles with changing values.

This week difficult planetary aspects may have you keeping your head under the bed covers, but it's okay to relax; there are positive moments too. Much of this will play out on the world stage, but you may also have personal events occur now. Use keen observation and awareness to guide you through the next couple of weeks.

It's a relief to get some good news and have hope for the future at the beginning of the week. But shifts will arrive, and a time of volatility follows. The shifts at hand involve an ongoing conflict between ideals of equality and desires to maintain personal property and status. You'll see this on the world stage and must work to keep things calm and balanced in your personal and outer life.

At the New Moon in Capricorn on the 13th it may be hard to resolve divisions. Seek ways to bring peace to your heart during this powerful intention-setting time. You may soon experience a shift in both finances and what you value. Get practical help handling this if you need to.

This stressful week ends with more surprising shifts. Be open to expanding your perspective. You may find a change that works now or (hang in there) may work later.

Shadow:
Don't engage in the energy of struggle. Trying to break through locked doors brings suffering and potential injury. Choose peace and allow the time to pass knowing better times will come.

JANUARY 18-24

Lunar Signs:
PISCES, ARIES, TAURUS, GEMINI
Lunar Cycle:
FIRST QUARTER, SECOND QUARTER

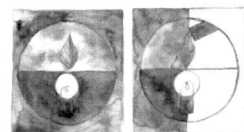

Sun enters Aquarius, Mercury trine North Node empowering humanitarian thoughts of the future. Wednesday Mars conjunct Uranus can trigger an angry personal or social revolution. Saturday Mars square Jupiter, Venus sextile Neptune indicates that conflict between possession and sharing may be softened by compassion. Sunday's Sun conjunct Saturn empowers a group leader.

While the conflicts continue, the Sun leaves practical Capricorn, entering free-thinking Aquarius on the 19th. On Wednesday, the revolutionary aspect of Aquarius arrives as a volatile moment. The tension of this Mars conjunct Uranus in Taurus is felt from the 18th through the 23rd. Conflicts between expansion and a desire to preserve the status quo are not easily resolved. Let the tension dissolve and stay open-minded.

Self-expression and identity are now highlighted as the sun sits in Aquarius. You'll notice an emphasis on the future, groups, friendships, independence, freedom, intuition, and the importance of energy. For many, frustration may reach the breaking point this week as shocking news continues to provoke polarized attitudes. Wisdom favors keeping a cool head and using intuition to read what's happening in your surroundings. Do your best to avoid being drawn into conflict.

♡ Suns, Moons, and Success. Learn more: www.ChooseBigChange.com ♡

It is also a good time to monitor your own energy levels. It is not a time to push for things, engage in arguments, or launch something new. Work on feeling grounded and centered.

Saturday afternoon and evening brings a welcome shift into soft, spiritual, and creative energy. It's a good night for a romantic candlelight dinner, music, and dance. Sunday you can seek ways to manifest your hopes and dreams.

Shadow:
There's a high potential to overreact and overdo it this week. Open to receiving creative input and spiritual direction at week's end.

JANUARY 25-31

Lunar Signs:
GEMINI, CANCER, LEO, VIRGO
Lunar Cycle:
2ND QUARTER, FULL, 3RD QUARTER

Sun square Uranus may bring conflict over future and finance. Venus conjunct Pluto and Leo Full Moon inspires intense feelings about relationship and career. The Sun conjunct Jupiter brings an uplifting optimism as Mercury retrogrades in Aquarius, and the mind internalizes for review.

You may feel like you're driving with one foot on the gas and one on the brake at the beginning of the week when surprises require a quick detour on your path. A sudden change may upset your plans. As midweek approaches, some relief may arrive if you've been preparing yourself for The Age of Aquarius (reference the 2021 illustration about Age of Aquarius). Feelings intensify for the dramatic Full Moon in Leo on Thursday. Work to maintain focus as Mercury slows to retrograde in Aquarius on the 30th.

Two positive days arrive at the Leo Full Moon. You can reap rewards, have successful meetings, and make or deepen an important connection. As Mercury slows down before its three-week retrograde, focus, prioritize tasks, and get as much done on projects as possible.

Begin now to review January's events. Explore and acknowledge what you've learned about how to deal with current issues. Prepare for the potential conflicts of the Saturn Uranus squares that will occur later this year.

(Publisher suggestion: reread the introduction to this year's astrology in the front of the book.)

Shadow:
Avoid letting mind and body seesaw from one extreme to another as it is weakening in every way. Practice techniques for balance and coordination.

January Moons

NEW MOON IN 23° CAPRICORN
JANUARY 13 00:58 AM EST

This New Moon supports intentions for the Capricorn areas of career, achievement, public life, status, structures, methods, and timing for success. The Sun and Moon join Pluto, creating intensity in both feelings and self-expression that can verge on obsession.

You may experience volatility as part of the conflict between a vision of a more humane future and the passion for holding on to personal property. There is a flow of uncertainty and change as Mars in Taurus squares Saturn in Aquarius.

Neptune in Pisces square both nodal axes which are currently Sagittarius (south) and Gemini (north). Oh, such astro-speak! *(Refer to the section in the front of the Almanac for more information about nodes.)* These movements of the nodes squaring a spiritual planet like Neptune directs you to look within for the very conflicts you see in the outer world. You are urged to apply compassion to those involved in heavy situations. You may swing between a desire for change and the fear of it. You'll be okay; seek solid ground. Peaceful understanding comes when you let go of beliefs, seek more information, and filter all through spiritual guidance.

FULL MOON IN 9° LEO
JANUARY 28 2:16 PM EST

Full Moons represent the Sun opposite the Moon. Oppositions bring tension no matter which planets or signs they are occurring in. Every opposition suggests a need for balance by finding the middle ground, but the two fixed signs at play under this Full Moon, Leo and Aquarius, have a hard time letting go to do this. The difference between the need for attention, affection, loyalty, and self-expression (Leo Moon) competes with detached observation, independence, friendship, and group affiliation (Aquarius Sun). Everything is coming to a head. Key players, Saturn and Jupiter, are positioned for additional tension and will pull strongly toward the Aquarius point of view. Think: Forward-thinking, group-oriented, humanitarian topics.

You might find yourself stuck in the aftereffect of conflicts already passed and having a hard time finding your way out. If something (or someone) has to go in order for the situation to resolve, now's the time for release. Detached objectivity will assist as you do your processing. Keep creating your vision, even if some adjustments need to be made. It's a good time to give peace a chance.

♡ Suns, Moons, and Success. Learn more: www.ChooseBigChange.com ♡

Energy Almanac 2021 Edition

Page 27

123 Numerology

A 6 month in a 5 year, January 2021 is fueled with nurturing energy and a desire to act on others' behalf. More than ever you will be moved to serve family and listen to other people's problems. The 6 energy sends vibrations of love and joy toward those you care about. You may find yourself noticing the beauty that surrounds you. Be receptive this month as it carries the abundant rewards of past efforts that are available. What a beautiful way to embrace the energy of the year 2021.

Gemstones

AMAZONITE

Amazonite is a gorgeous blue-green stone with tones that vary from light milky blue to deep sea green. It gets its name from the Amazon River. Amazonite is a gentle and powerful stone that activates both the heart and throat chakras. Amazonite can help balance our emotions by keeping us in touch with our truth. It enhances not only inner peace but peace with others through opening the heart chakra. By stimulating the throat chakra, we are able to more easily express our truth and communicate. It is a great stone for meditation and breathwork. Be sure to use these stones during times of change, chaos, or frustration. Harnessing the water element, this amazing stone is great for gaining clarity and releasing fears.

Keywords: TRUTH, HARMONY, COMMUNICATION, AND PEACE.
Mantra: I SPEAK MY TRUTH TO OTHERS AND TO THE UNIVERSE.

Essential Oils

The energy of January 2021 is inviting us to find balance. We need to call upon our resilience as this month may be a bit of an emotional rollercoaster. Given that the energies of January could be volatile at times, the oils chosen for this month can keep us grounded and calm as we navigate our emotions and temper our reactions. This month may prove to be both physically and emotionally taxing. Consistent use of these oils will provide us with the added support we need.

FOR TOPICAL USE

Spikenard: Apply 1-2 drops on the insides of wrists and/or over solar plexus. Spikenard is used to encourage calm, centering, balance, and resolution.

Cedarwood: Apply 1-2 drops to the bottom of each foot. Cedarwood encourages strength, focus, balance, fortitude, persistence, and protectiveness. It assists us in looking forward into the future with strength and the bringing together of community.

DIFFUSE THIS BLEND

- **Lemon 3 drops**
- **Rosemary 2 drops**
- **Ginger 1 drop**
- **Rose 1 drop**

This aromatic blend is all about lifting spirits. Lemon aids in focus while Rosemary supports you in receiving new experiences. Ginger encourages optimism and Rose holds the highest vibration of all essential oils on the planet. It's a powerful healer and encourages joy and happiness. Remember: *Love always wins!*

Yoga

CULTIVATING A MEDITATION PRACTICE

It's a new year on the calendar. But the cycles of the earth prompt something deep and ancient in us: a knowing that the light of the sun will always return and bring us warmth, only to be proceeded by cold and wet days once again. It's this cycle that reminds us of the cyclical nature of existence.

Deep into winter in the northern hemisphere, we seek out warm, fuzzy blankets and hot tea. And in the southern hemisphere, where the sun has just reached its zenith in the sky, it's a time to recognize our earthly bounty with grace and moderation.

Whether we are in the depth of winter, or in the heat of summer, a turn to our yoga practice can help us to find grounding and inner peace within these zenith seasons. For many, January is time to turn in, reflect, and take pause. Sometimes, especially in areas of the northern hemisphere, we are guided by Mother Nature to stay in due to the snow and cold; to be gentle and nourish ourselves and our family in the warmth of the home. How can we cultivate this turning in with our yoga practice? One way is through meditation.

Today, yoga asana is all the rage. But rarely do yoga practices in studios or home also include a meditation practice. Traditionally, the practice of hatha yoga, along with pranayama (breathing exercises) was used by yogis to ready the body for long periods of sitting, with the end result of meditation being Samādhi (literally liberation and bliss). This is also known as spiritual awakening or enlightenment. Meditation is the gateway.

Take some time this month to learn the different meditation practices available to compliment your yoga practice. One easy meditation practice you can try right now is Circulation Breath Meditation.

CIRCULATION BREATH MEDITATION

1. Find a quiet place where you can sit with your spine fully erect.

2. Place each of your hands, palm down on your thighs, feeling your alignment with your body as you do so.

3. Calm your mind by first breathing in deeply, holding your breath for three seconds and breathing out gently through your mouth. Repeat three times.

4. On the next inhalation of breath, bring your attention to the base of your spine and, as you breathe in slowly, imagine energy flowing up your spine with your inhalation. End your inhalation as you reach your top lip. With your exhalation, see the energy follow the front of your body starting with your bottom lip and ending the exhalation at the bottom of your spine.

5. Each full circulation of breath, from bottom of spine and back again, is one count. Repeat the circulation of breath 20 times. (If you lose your count, start over again.) Over time you will see your concentration increase.

♡ Suns, Moons, and Success. Learn more: www.ChooseBigChange.com ♡

Page 29

Chew on This

Digestion begins the second we put food in our mouth. There are digestive enzymes in our saliva that begin to break down our food as we chew. When we chew more thoroughly, we increase nutrient absorption. Saliva also neutralizes our food, making for smoother digestion and, for most of us, less gas!

One way to chew mindfully is to count your chews in each bite. Aim for 30 chews per bite before swallowing. It can be helpful to put down your utensils between bites so you can focus on chewing.

Stock your fridge with neutralizing and alkaline foods as these foods also help the internal processes such as our respiratory and urinary systems.

We suggest:
- Sweet potatoes
- Brussel sprouts
- Cabbage
- Cauliflower
- Tangerines
- Grapefruit
- Almonds

BAKED BREAKFAST GRAPEFRUIT

Slice a large grapefruit in half, place the open side up in a baking dish, drizzle lightly with a tablespoon or less of local raw honey, sprinkle with sea salt, and bake for 15 minutes at 350 degrees. For easier eating, slice along each wedge using a sharp steak knife before pulling the "meat" out of the pith.

Health Hint

Start your year off right with good pico-ionic magnesium which opens the cells so they can better absorb the vitamins and minerals you'll take this year. Magnesium facilitates at least 1000 different enzyme processes within the body. This excellent mineral often alleviates migraines and can assist with heartbeat issues. Follow the instructions on the label for proper dosage.

Notes

_____

_____

_____

_____

_____

_____

_____

_____

_____

_____

_____

_____

_____

_____

_____

_____

_____

_____

_____

_____

_____

_____

_____

_____

♡ Suns, Moons, and Success. Learn more: www.ChooseBigChange.com ♡

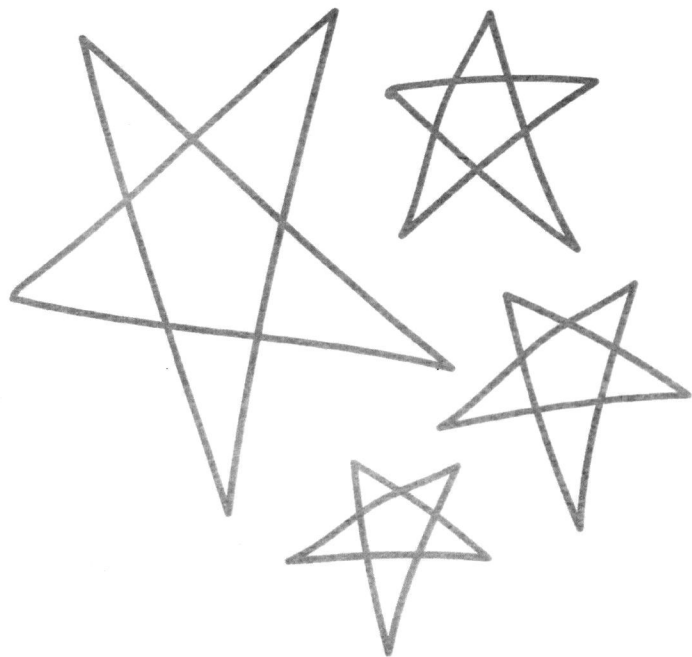

February

FREEDOM, FINANCE, FUTURE

FEBRUARY 1-7

Do seek silence and solitude.
Do not hold on too tightly to your own ideas.

FEBRUARY 8-14

Do expect a breakthrough.
Do not lock in your plan; stay flexible.

FEBRUARY 15-21

Do add structure to your goals.
Do not be averse to new ways of thinking.

FEBRUARY 22-28

Do listen for intuitive information.
Do not avoid feeling.

Let Silence

TAKE YOU TO THE core OF LIFE.

WHAT SPACE CAN I BE TO RECEIVE MONEY WITH EASE?

FEBRUARY 11

NEW MOON IN 23° AQUARIUS
Love and The Good of All

FEBRUARY 27

FULL MOON IN 8° VIRGO
Ending Perfectionism

February

Solar Cycle:
1ST QUARTER
Keywords:
FREEDOM, FINANCE, FUTURE

February begins with Mercury retrograde in Aquarius where we may experience a general mayhem when we internalize our thoughts. Utilize this time for all things with "re" (restoring, reviewing, renovating). It's the perfect time to review thoughts and communication around friendships, groups, and hopes for the future. Mercury goes direct on the 20th.

This month also brings the first of this year's powerful squares from Saturn in Aquarius to Uranus in Taurus. You can expect tension between tradition and innovation as it asks you to reconsider new goals and form new values in the area of money and possessions.

Venus will spend most of the month in lively, independent Aquarius. Early in the month disappointment and surprising changes dampen the mood and outlook, but the good news is by mid-month, experiences could prove memorable in a very positive way. Things, in general, are looking up, and something you've hoped for is delivered. Memories of exciting times and words of love combine with a desire to give romantic gifts and enjoy dreamy dinners. Cozy up to your boo, even if it's the person you see in the mirror every morning. Optimism combined with a spirit of fun and humor may lead to hopeful discussions about the future. Venus also rules money, and things can prove fruitful in that realm too. One caveat—while Mercury is retrograde, don't plan for the future or sign contractual agreements.

A glitch between Venus and Mars may involve differences in financial planning or someone being too possessive. After the Sun shifts into Pisces on the 18th, the solar rays bestow empathy and feelings of gentle concern. You can easily resolve differences by responding to others with sensitivity. Mercury's direct motion on the 20th also helps you communicate clearly and move forward with important decisions or purchases.

Venus enters Pisces on the 25th, bringing the potential for compassion and unconditional love, but be on guard against seeking escape in fantasy, over-idealizing others, and taking on wounded birds. Sun, Uranus, and Jupiter will make changes easy and keep optimism high. Their positive presence is on board for the Full Moon on the 27th.

DATES TO WATCH:

- **February 1 Sun square Mars and Venus enters Aquarius.** Freedom lovers may experience conflict with those passionate about acquisition and ownership.

- **February 6 Venus conjunct Saturn, square Uranus.** The flow of love and finance meets obstacles, disappointment, and surprising change.

- **February 11 New Moon and Venus conjunct Jupiter.** We seed intentions for the coming month with love and optimism as a wish comes true. *See February Moons section.*

- **February 13-14 Mercury conjunct Venus, Mars sextile Neptune, Mercury conjunct Jupiter, Venus trine North Node.** Joyful communications and sensitive actions add to positive aspirations for the future.

- **February 17-19 Saturn squares Uranus, Sun enters Pisces, Venus squares Mars.** Tension from events in the outer and personal world require change. Sensitivity heightens and conflict forms.

- **February 20 Mercury stations direct.** Our communication and connection to others may begin to improve.

- **February 24-25 Mars trine Pluto, Jupiter trine North Node.** Material matters feel under control and optimism is at hand.

- **February 27 Virgo Full Moon.** *See February Moons section.*

Suns, Moons, and Success. Learn more: www.ChooseBigChange.com

Energy Almanac 2021 EDITION

Page 35

FEBRUARY ASTROLOGY BY THE WEEKS

<table>
<tr><td>

FEBRUARY 1-7

</td><td>

Lunar Signs:
LIBRA, SCORPIO, SAGITTARIUS, CAPRICORN
Lunar Cycle:
3RD QUARTER, 4TH QUARTER

</td></tr>
</table>

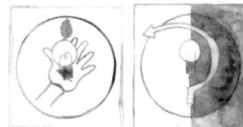

Sun square Mars and Venus enters Aquarius impacting independence versus possession and a shift in your love nature. On Friday Sun trines North Node offering opportunity for open-minded meetings. Saturday Venus conjunct Saturn, so watch for disappointment. Sunday Venus square Uranus. Be sure to allow for shifts and rifts.

February begins with a challenge to your goals because someone is resisting change. As internal values shift to new areas, there could be more conflicts ahead. Rest up. A few days of quiet may help you expect a reliable outcome.

On Saturday two possible scenarios show up. Something is denied and hope is lost, or a sudden feeling of safety is found. A reversal arrives on Sunday regarding the foundations of the situation, and it's particularly related to finance, possession and what you value.

Shadow:
Pushing too hard for personal values or expecting others to be on board with future goals that seem to threaten foundations won't always work. Don't over-identify with either side to relieve tension and allow the unfolding.

<table>
<tr><td>

FEBRUARY 8-14

</td><td>

Lunar Signs:
CAPRICORN, AQUARIUS, PISCES, ARIES
Lunar Cycle:
4TH QUARTER, NEW, 1ST QUARTER

</td></tr>
</table>

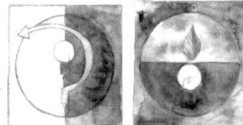

Sun conjunct Mercury, identifying with thoughts. Mercury square Mars, arguments. Thursday, Mercury trine North Node, Venus conjunct Jupiter, Aquarius New Moon, a breakthrough and a new start. Saturday, Mercury conjunct Venus, words of love. Sunday Mars sextile Neptune, Venus trine North Node, Mercury conjunct Jupiter, all bring visions of happiness.

If you and a friend, partner, or significant other can be open to seeing things from a new perspective, differences will resolve and be replaced by positive interactions. Finally, there is a restoration of optimism for the future. A personal relationship blossoms and the next level is discussed.

Apply your intuition this week and take practical steps regarding finances. Bask in the enjoyment of a life well lived on Sunday. It's the perfect day to celebrate.

Since Mercury is still in retrograde, some new plans for the future will change in an unexpected way. This is not the time to sign on any dotted lines, unless the situation has been in negotiation since before the Mercury retrograde began on January 30th. Remember, too, the coming Saturn Uranus square will bring challenges and sudden shifts.

Shadow:
With a focus on positive thoughts for the future, you may forget this beneficial time isn't locked in forever. Take time to reflect on how your own energy created these good outcomes so this can be utilized toward creating positivity in the future.

✷ www.TheEnergyAlmanac.com ✷

FEBRUARY 15-21

Lunar Signs:
ARIES, TAURUS, GEMINI, CANCER
Lunar Cycle:
1ST QUARTER, 2ND QUARTER

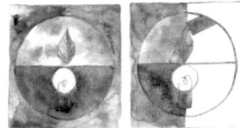

Saturn squares Uranus and you may face changing plans. Thursday, Sun enters Pisces and there is a new emotional sensitivity afoot. Friday Venus squares Mars creating a battle between freedom and possession. Saturday Mercury goes direct in Aquarius and you can begin to see things from a new perspective.

An abrupt change from last week may bring tension and conflict over matters in the outer and personal world. Your differences could be hard to reconcile. Extra effort is needed to break a stalemate. You begin to move forward with new thinking.

The first of this year's three important Saturn Uranus squares arrives as the week begins.

Saturn in Aquarius begs for structure concerning our future goals. Uranus, planet of upheaval and change, is in Taurus, the sign of personal finance and values. When these planets square one another, these topics come to a head. The natural tension that occurs during this time period may be felt within your relationships. While others may like the status quo, you may thrive on what's new and innovative. In the outer world you may see groups standing up for change warring against others who cling to what they've deemed reliable and steadfast. You'll surely see which side you're on. Do your best to seek neutrality as you explain your side.

Mercury now goes direct in Aquarius and reveals to you your new thoughts and perspectives on friends, groups, and goals. You're probably eager to begin acting on them.

Shadow:
Refuse to engage in the energy of struggle. Don't let outer circumstances destroy inner peace. Trust the winds of change, knowing better times are ahead.

FEBRUARY 22-28

Lunar Signs:
CANCER, LEO, VIRGO, LIBRA
Lunar Cycle:
2ND QUARTER, FULL, 3RD QUARTER

Late in the week Mars trine Pluto, Venus enters Pisces, Sun sextile Uranus, and Jupiter trine North Node creates action with compassion. Positive information and intuition prevail. Saturday's Virgo Full Moon seeks compromise between the spiritual and the mundane.

Things settle down and hope returns along with a sense of greater stability this week. These positive aspects are also active in this week's Full Moon in Virgo.

Use good will, humor, and optimism to build relationships this week. Check in. What can you do to preserve the solid foundations in your life? If you'll be using them in the future, now is a good time to consider any needed transformation.

You are on your way to realizing your goals and, if your goals will also benefit others, you will find doorways opening that support you. At the Full Moon, gather all your tools and use the bright moonlight to see the way ahead.

Shadow:
Be mindful of not relying only on electronic communication. Be in touch with the physical world and your emotional feelings.

♡ Suns, Moons, and Success. Learn more: www.ChooseBigChange.com ♡

Energy Almanac 2021 Edition

Page 37

February Moons

NEW MOON IN 23° AQUARIUS
FEBRUARY 11 2:05 PM EST

This New Moon is the time to set intentions for the areas of friendship, group affiliations, hopes and goals for the future, money from career, intuition, and understanding energy. Six planets and an asteroid in Aquarius will give an extraordinary emphasis to all of these life areas. All planets are in an unusually tight group between late Capricorn and mid-Taurus. This will keep you occupied in specific areas and having to seek balance because many of these planets have aspects of stubborn conflict.

Sun and Moon are joined with asteroid Pallas Athena (wisdom warrior) and the planet Mercury which accelerates communications and instinctive feelings. Use this quickening to focus on the future and your aspirations for freedom and all things group oriented. You may feel a deep passion to keep things grounded and preserve personal worth and possessions.

Saturn in Aquarius bestows lessons and can suggest good methods and timing for you, but it is square Uranus in Taurus. Apply innovation (Uranus) to the purely physical world of Taurus. Think money, home, food, and aesthetics. Expect ease once this tight group of planets in Aquarius begins to break up later in the month. It is safe to feel optimism as Mercury joins Venus and Jupiter. These planets value the Aquarian ideals, bring gifts, and expand consciousness in these areas. The message for this moon: Seek balance.

FULL MOON IN 8° VIRGO
FEBRUARY 27 3:17 AM EST

The difference between Virgo's need for perfection and organization bumps up against identifying with sensitivity and spirituality, a Piscean trait. This comes to a head while the Moon in Virgo opposes the Sun in Pisces.

Every opposition (full moons are always oppositions) suggests the need for balance by finding the middle ground. The Virgo Moon is with asteroid Vesta (protector of the hearth and what we value most), while the Sun is with Venus in Pisces. This moon offers you the potential for compassion and unconditional love and for creating a natural desire to help others.

Fortunately, the practical, organizing instincts of the Virgo Moon are trine Uranus in Taurus. This lunar influence makes you open and able to accommodate change and insights about money, diet, health, home, and even nature itself.

There's a lovely aspect at play. Use your intuition (Pisces) about future financial flows to find workable solutions (Virgo) to changes that arise. Use the passion and power of Taurus/Mars trine Pluto in Capricorn for pursuing goals with workable methods. Renovate when necessary. You could surely experience optimism and gather needed information for moving forward.

There is still an uncomfortable but necessary lesson to learn from this moment. Allow the unfolding.

723 Numerology

A 7 month in a 5 year. Look within for all your answers to produce a life of vitality. Stay focused on how the answers to your questions are found within. Being driven by emotions will push you further from your goals. This is not the time to force anything to happen in your life. Allow the flow of the universe to supply you with everything you want. You will not have the urge to be social this month. If you do find yourself at a social gathering, you will be around those who are spiritual in nature and who will send you vibes of optimism and comfort.

Gemstones

ROSE QUARTZ

Rose Quartz is a gentle, semi-translucent pink stone. It is the ultimate stone of love. It activates the heart center of the wearer, as well as connecting you to the heart of the earth and the heart of the Universe. With Venus in Aquarius and in Pisces in February, Rose Quartz will balance, heal, and cultivate feelings, compassion, and unconditional love. By stimulating the heart chakra, Rose Quartz can contribute ease to not only our social relationships but also to our inner world and peace. This is an incredible stone for meditation. Be sure to use it regularly to expand your self-love, allowance, and compassion for others. Harnessing the water element, this amazing stone is great for enhancing fluidity, acknowledging that we are all connected, and healing emotions.

Keywords: LOVE, RELEASING STRESS, EMOTIONAL HEALING, GENTLENESS AND UNION WITH ONENESS.
Mantra: MY HEART RADIATES LOVE FOR MYSELF, OTHERS, THE EARTH, AND THE UNIVERSE.

Essential Oils

This month we are being asked to bring attention to our thoughts and communications surrounding our relationships and our hopes for the future. We will be faced with having to confront what is no longer serving us and what we need to let go of. In order to do this, there will be an increased need for harmony and balance as we navigate through the month.

FOR TOPICAL USE

Patchouli: Apply 1-2 drops at the base of spine or bottom of the feet. A calming and grounding oil. A powerful attractor of love and money.

Lavender: This calming oil is used to aid us in communication. Apply to the throat and on the bottom of the feet. Use 1-2 drops.

DIFFUSE THIS BLEND

- **Lime 3 drops**
- **Lemongrass 2 drops**
- **Douglas Fir 2 drops**
- **Lavender 1 drop**

To revitalize and balance between the heart and the mind, start with Lime. Lemongrass is a powerful cleanser physically, emotionally, and mentally, aiding you in letting go of things that are not serving you. Douglas Fir provides grounding and assists in opening the mind to see the gift of new growth while Lavender is comforting to the heart and calming to the emotions.

INGESTIBLE OPTIONS

Lime or Lemongrass: Either of these oils are great options to add to cold water. The benefit of Lime is its ability to revitalize you while Lemongrass is a fabulous cleanser.

♡ Suns, Moons, and Success. Learn more: www.ChooseBigChange.com ♡

Energy Almanac 2021 EDITION

Page 39

Yoga

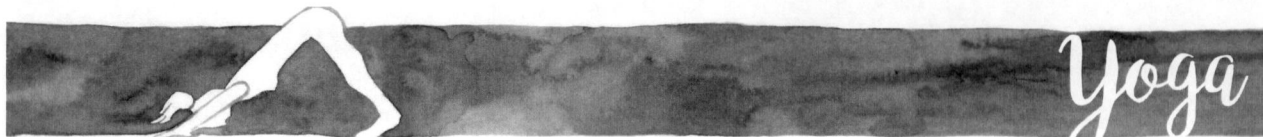

TRATAKA GAZING

trāṭaka: "look, gaze"

Trataka gazing is an ancient tantric yoga purification method used to help activate deeper spiritual awareness. By gazing with one-pointed attention at an object, black dot, or candle flame, the pineal gland, a small pea-sized gland in the center of the brain, may become energized, thereby activating the third eye.

Mystics and some spiritual traditions consider the pineal gland, (which is energetically connected to the third eye), the key to unlock your connection between the physical and spiritual worlds. With a healthy and awakened pineal gland and third eye, clear spiritual vision and direction can be obtained.

Besides finding inner balance, many practitioners have discovered that they increase their physical balance in their daily life. When life throws you a curve, you can find your inner balance and calm concentration.

TRATAKA GAZING EXERCISE

1. Start your practice by finding a quiet place where you will not be disturbed. Select an object to gaze at such as a candle flame or black dot on a white background that you can place in front of you. You may choose to sit in silence or with some soft music in the background as long as it will not be a disturbance.

2. Set a timer for ten minutes to start. You can try for longer periods of time after mastering ten minutes of uninterrupted concentration.

3. Find a comfortable sitting position and with eyelids and eyes relaxed, stare at the object with unwavering attention. A good way to master attention is to silently repeat a mantra to yourself such as, "I am at peace", or any other mantra that will allow you to meld completely into the moment. If you allow your attention to waver away from the object and into your thought processes, come back to the object. Know that with practice, this will become easier.

4. After practicing Trataka Gazing for some time, you will notice that your attention in everyday life, such as when driving or cooking, will become more immediate and in the moment. Your reflexes may become heightened as well as you learn to stay completely in the present moment.

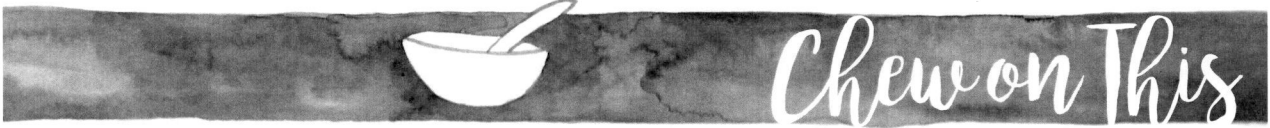

Chew on This

Choose foods this month that calm and ground you. Sweet vegetables ease the internal organs of the body and invigorate the mind. Many "sweet vegetables" are root vegetables and are typically in abundance and easy to find this time of year. They are energetically grounding, help the body maintain blood sugar levels, reduce sweet cravings, and break down animal foods in the body.

We suggest trying a variety of:

- Carrots (purple, yellow, and orange)
- Winter squashes (butternut, acorn, and spaghetti)
- Beets
- Parsnips
- Red Radishes

GROUNDING SOUP

- One large onion, peeled and cut into bite-size pieces
- Your favorite root vegetables, washed, peeled, diced into bite-size chunks

In a medium-size pot, add just enough water or stock to cover the vegetables. Add more water as needed while cooking. Simmer until vegetables are at the desired softness. The softer the vegetable, the sweeter. Once cooked to your liking, serve in bowls, season, and enjoy!

Save and drink the leftover cooking water as it is a soothing and healing tonic by itself!

Health Hint

The average person uses up their personal mineral reserves through stress and blood loss. Because soils we grow food in are depleted and no longer contain the rich bounty they used to, our natural mineral intake is low. Liquid ionic minerals will give your body the building blocks it needs to keep you healthy. These are especially necessary for women planning a pregnancy. Take the recommended dosage on the label of the product.

♡ Suns, Moons, and Success. Learn more: www.ChooseBigChange.com ♡

Page 41

Notes

—◇◇◇—

_____

_____

_____

_____

_____

_____

_____

_____

_____

_____

_____

_____

_____

_____

_____

_____

_____

_____

_____

_____

_____

_____

_____

_____

_____

_____

Grab your free bonuses here: www.ChooseBigChange.com/bonus21

✫ www.TheEnergyAlmanac.com ✫

March

CREATIVITY, ACTION, MANIFESTATION

MARCH 1-7

Do be clear in your communications.
Do not engage in intense reactions.

MARCH 8-14

Do spend time in creative visioning.
Do not be caught up in illusion.

MARCH 15-21

Do watch for surprises in money and values.
Do not stay stuck in foggy thinking.

MARCH 22-28

Do be mindful of timing.
Do not allow conflicts to cause doubt.

MARCH 29- APRIL 4

Do pay good attention to timing.
Do not get caught in a cycle of self-doubt.

when you practice *loving kindness & compassion* you are the first one to profit.

WHAT IN MY LIFE FEELS GENERATIVE AND CREATIVE?

MARCH 13

NEW MOON IN 23° PISCES
Retreat and Listen

MARCH 28

FULL MOON IN 8° LIBRA
Restoring balance

♡ Love the Energy Almanac? Share on social media: #EnergyAlmanac ♡

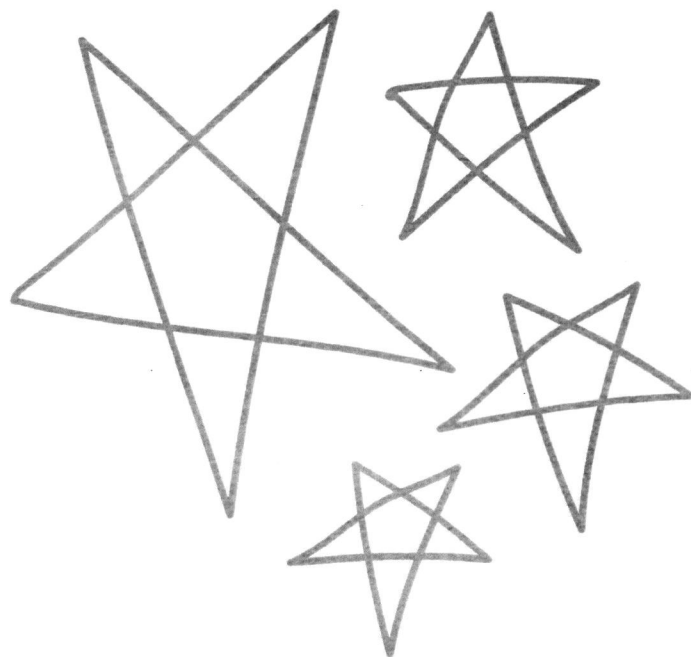

March

◇◇◇

Solar Cycle:
1ST QUARTER
Keywords:
CREATIVITY, ACTION MANIFESTATION

This month all planets are in direct motion, and the midpoint of the waxing solar cycle arrives with the Spring Equinox. It's time now to take action and nurture your projects and goals. Your creative focus and values move from the inner world to the outer. Mars, Jupiter, Saturn, and Mercury in air signs will provide you the needed objectivity. Use this inspired intellectual energy to keep you from drifting away in dreams during the first two weeks of the month. Afterward, allow the Mercury energy to supply you with the mental stimulus for action. You will notice a heightened sense of intellect, thought, and communications in March due to Mars (action) in Gemini (thinking). Top that with Mercury entering Pisces giving us more "feelings". It's a highly intuitive time, too, and meditation will bring you helpful, inspiring messages. Notice an increased love for action, competition, and exploring. Use that energy toward achieving goals.

DATES TO WATCH:

- **March 3-5 Venus sextile Uranus, Mercury trine Jupiter, Mars enters Gemini.** Creative inspiration, expanded consciousness, active communications.

- **March 11 Sun conjunct Neptune.** Fantasy and potential self-deception.

- **March 13 Pisces New Moon.** Lower energy supports retreat and dreaming.

- **March 14 Venus conjunct Neptune.** Creative works, compassion, or illusions occur now.

- **March 15 Mercury enters Pisces.** Thinking becomes sensitive and intuitive.

- **March 20 Sun enters Aries, Spring Equinox.** Energy grows as the 2nd Solar Quarter begins.

- **March 21 Venus enters Aries.** Values and how we love shifts.

- **March 24-25 Mercury square Mars, Mercury square the Nodes.** Irritation impedes cooperative efforts.

- **March 29-30 Mercury conjunct Neptune, Venus sextile Saturn, Libra Full Moon.** Inner guidance or illusion; action on future plans, friendships, and group relationships.

♡ Suns, Moons, and Success. Learn more: www.ChooseBigChange.com ♡

MARCH ASTROLOGY BY THE WEEKS

MARCH 1-7

Lunar Signs:
LIBRA, SCORPIO, SAGITTARIUS, CAPRICORN
Lunar Cycle:
3RD QUARTER, 4TH QUARTER

Mercury trine the North Node stimulates exploration. Venus sextile Uranus and Mars enters Gemini bring you changes and activity. Mercury conjunction Jupiter, Sun square North Node signals good news and optimism.

A Lot can be gained from a new perspective, and you can now seek innovative ways to create helpful changes. As your mind starts accelerating, plan to celebrate because good news is on the way. Staying grounded in reality could be the real problem.

In the lunar 3rd Quarter, you'll be anxious to share revelations and new information with others. Who wouldn't be? This is a time of inspired creativity that can be applied to new art forms and/or mundane matters, like finance, real estate and body care. If you notice you're experiencing an active mind, be careful. With Mars fiery energy at play, do stay alert. Attitudes may intensify and you will want to hold off on any desire to express anger, either verbally or in writing. Conversely, if you're on the receiving end, practice objectivity and don't engage. Good news, happy conversations, and uplifting meetings are due to arrive by Friday which also makes it a good day to network and market.

Stay clear in your communications and ask for inner guidance if you feel torn between two perspectives. Look at the events of the past two weeks to discover what may need to change. Review all areas of your life.

Shadow:
Too much time in dreaming and thinking of the future while ignoring mundane tasks and needs of the body can create real upset. Ground your ideas with a list of steps you'll take to achieve the future you're thinking of.

MARCH 8-14

Lunar Signs:
CAPRICORN, AQUARIUS, PISCES, ARIES
Lunar Cycle:
4TH QUARTER, NEW, 1ST QUARTER

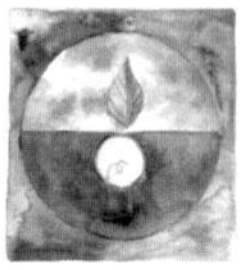

A few days of quiet end Tuesday when Venus squares the nodes. You may discover that love doesn't take sides. The Sun conjuncts Neptune and there is potential for self-illusion. Saturday holds the Pisces New Moon with a slower energy. Sunday Venus joins Neptune making it a good time for dreams of love.

With Pisces Sun, Moon, Venus, and Neptune joined at the time of the New Moon, you are in a highly receptive mode that supports positive vision, compassion, creative and spiritual work. But watch for Piscean behavior of illusion and fantasy. Fortunately, there are four planets in logical, analytical, objective air signs, including those of the mind and motivation, so pull on their energy if the fantasy balloon rises too far away from you.

Shadow:
Be wary of not being able to tell fact from fantasy which can, in the end, lead you astray.

MARCH 15-21

Lunar Signs:
ARIES, TAURUS, GEMINI, CANCER
Lunar Cycle:
1ST QUARTER, 2ND QUARTER

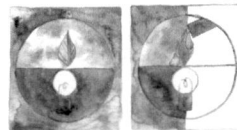

Mercury enters Pisces and your thoughts become hazy. Sun sextile Pluto on Tuesday and Venus sextile Pluto on Thursday offer an anchoring structure. Saturday the Sun enters Aries and the Spring Equinox is upon us. Sunday Venus enters Aries and Mercury sextile Uranus.

When you allow feelings and psychic receptivity to monitor the news and inform your ideas, things will begin to flow in a way that is positive this week. Who can you contact for advice? They may be the key to making your dreams a manageable reality. Seek a guide or mentor.

You may shift into action as we enter this 2nd Solar Quarter. Note how action speeds up at the Spring Equinox. Innovation and inspired solutions for change are afoot. Keep your eyes open for surprises in the realm of finance, real estate, and values.

Shadow:
Don't fail to seek wise guidance or you may lose an opportunity to reassess and repair any weak places in your plans. Experience has great value. Find someone who has been there, done that.

MARCH 22-28

Lunar Signs:
CANCER, LEO, VIRGO, LIBRA
Lunar Cycle:
2ND QUARTER, FULL

Mars trine Saturn brings together action and wisdom. Mercury square Mars, if left unattended, can cause arguments. Mercury squares the nodes creating indecision. The Sun conjunct Venus is about self-love. Mars conjuncts North Node to provide help in finding the answer.

This week you'll find yourself working in an active, wise way to get things moving but, without clear information or a solid response, your impatience could win the day and lead to harsh words.

You may feel the need to protect your independence and sense of leadership. Relax. This is from old wounds. Sprinkle love into the situation, for yourself and others. Ultimately, the information and answers arrive, and things can move forward.

As your feelings and relationship issues intensify, you'll see they're right on time. Energy always builds as the Full Moon arrives. This time it's in the sign of Libra.

Shadow:
Beware of wanting to be in the driver's seat and speed things up. Trust in the perfect unfolding as you develop your patience.

♡ Suns, Moons, and Success. Learn more: www.ChooseBigChange.com ♡

Page 47

MARCH 29-31, APRIL 1-4

Lunar Signs:
LIBRA, SCORPIO
Lunar Cycle:
1ST QUARTER

Mercury conjunct Neptune and Venus sextile Saturn combines psychic input with wise action. Sun sextile Saturn means efforts are successful and the month ends with inspired thought and resolutions.

The last three days of March energetically open up so you can harness intuitive hits and receive psychic input. Stay aware of potential areas for deception or confusion.

It's wise for you to temper this week's activities with solid methods and right timing. Your creative expression and love of a challenge can work well with good advice. Ask a trusted resource for insight on how to reach future goals and resolve difficulties in the area of friendships or group affiliations.

The pace seems right; the timing seems right. It's a relief to finally feel on track.

Shadow:
Refuse to let recent conflicts cause doubt, fear, or a desire to escape into fantasy. Practice reaffirming goals and mantras and work toward releasing the negative voices.

March Moons

NEW MOON IN 23° PISCES
MARCH 13, 2021 5:21 AM EST

At the Pisces New Moon, you can set intentions for the areas of spirituality, inner life, unconscious patterns that hold us back. The effects of ancestral energy and dealings to do with people in confinement are also at hand.

The Sun and Moon are joined with Neptune and Venus in this New Moon. You'll be in a compassionate, idealistic, creative and romantic (Venus) mode. Energy is always lower at the New Moon and with this Pisces quartet of planets, now is a perfect time to fluff your best pillow and retreat, rest and dream. Allowing this can be more productive than you imagine because of other planetary interactions. A sweet sextile from other planets will help strengthen and ground this energy.

Aquarius-friendly planetary aspects can expand your consciousness and bring intuitive insight as Saturn in Aquarius keeps lessons, methods, and timing focused on group interaction, friends, and hopes for the future. You'll have a steady mind and lowered tension, at long last!

_____
_____
_____
_____

Grab your free bonuses here: www.ChooseBigChange.com/bonus21

FULL MOON IN 8° LIBRA
MARCH 28, 2021 2:48 PM EDT

This full moon is about the difference between the need for partnership, agreement, discussion (Libra), versus identification with self, independence, and action (Aries). It all comes to a head while the Moon in Libra opposes the Sun in Aries.

This Full Moon has other planets at play. Notice it may be difficult to bring everyone together for negotiations.

The Full Libra Moon is alone as the only planet in one half of the zodiac, while the Sun is with Venus and Chiron is in Aries. Libra rules relationship and tension is accentuated by the reactivation of old wounds. Where inside of a relationship were you denied freedom, authentic individuality and leadership in love, self-expression and creativity? This is an active vibration worth looking at. Bring it to the surface for healing.

Moon, Sun and Venus form positive aspects to both Saturn in Aquarius and Mars, conjunct the North Node in Gemini. This powerful positioning of planets suggests you should include an objective moderator in discussions to help you reach an agreeable solution.

Mercury and Neptune in dreamy Pisces benefit from the sextile to powerful Pluto in Capricorn. This helps you ground creative vision and can reduce any feelings of vulnerability or victimization.

Remember, your reality is influenced by your own energy vibration. Keep your thoughts and visions for the future in front of you and stay in desire. That is the proposal of Jupiter in Aquarius (expanded consciousness), which is an active energy under this month's Full Moon.

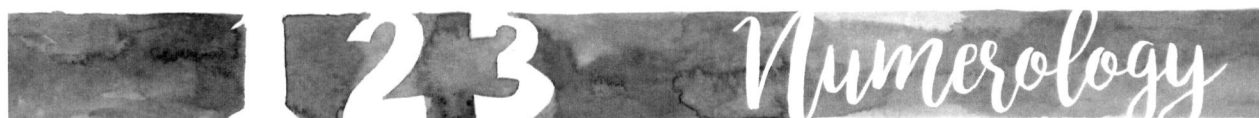

23 Numerology

An 8 month in a 5 year. The number 8 rules the material plane. If you have sown wisely you can have excellent manifestations. Approach every task this month with ambition. This is time to take action on any business plans you have been thinking about. Accelerate your manifestations by being efficient, organized, and adaptable. Remind yourself of your inner strength and avoid allowing external influences to deplete you. You have an abundance of resources with which to work, use it all wisely.

♡ Suns, Moons, and Success. Learn more: www.ChooseBigChange.com ♡

Energy Almanac 2021 EDITION

Page 49

Gemstones

TIGER EYE

Tiger Eye is a bold brown stone with bands of yellow-golden color reminiscent of a cat's eye (called chatoyancy). It is a powerful stone of vitality that activates the root chakra, second chakra and solar plexus. The combination of grounding energy with vitality inspires action. With Venus in Aries, we can cultivate a love of action and take our creativity beyond dreaming into actualization. By activating the first three chakras, Tiger Eye grounds us in our power. It also takes us out of judgment and paradox into the underlying unity of everything. This is a great stone for meditation. Use it to enhance your equilibrium and harmony with others. Harnessing the earth and fire elements, Tiger Eye is incredible for creativity and nurturing your priorities.

Keywords: ACTION, BALANCE BETWEEN EXTREMES, STRENGTH, AND PRACTICALITY
Mantra: I AM IN ALIGNMENT WITH CREATING MY GREATEST FUTURE.

Essential Oils

It's time to take action on the projects and goals we were thinking about last month. Let those creative juices flow and turn to your inner guidance. Use your best grounding practices to assist in staying focused.

FOR TOPICAL USE

Blue Tansy: Place 1-2 drops over the solar plexus or on the bottoms of each big toe. There is no better oil to support you in taking action than Blue Tansy. It will champion you when you are bumping up against resistance and aid you in focusing and taking action.

DIFFUSE THIS BLEND

- **Coriander 5 drops**
- **Geranium 3 drops**
- **Spearmint 3 drops**
- **Roman Chamomile 2 drops**
- **Blue Tansy 2 drops**

This fresh, light and floral blend will lift the March doldrums and provide courage, trust, and confidence as it eases your overactive mind. You won't feel as stuck either, as Blue Tansy will nudge you to move forward with focus.

INGESTIBLE OPTIONS

Cardamom: Known as the Oil of Objectivity, Cardamom will support you in clearing any confusion and aid you in clear thinking. Place 1 drop under the tongue, in a capsule, in water or tea. You may also enjoy its flavor when cooking.

Black Pepper: Black Pepper reignites your soul's fire and fuels motivation. Place 1 drop under the tongue, in a capsule or add to your favorite soup. It's important to note that when cooking with oils, they are very potent and less is more.

SURYA NAMASKAR:

Sun Salutation: *Sūrya*: "Sun"; *Namaskār*: Greeting

Spring in the northern hemisphere means the sun's path is higher in the sky, warming the earth and bringing abundance and activity. This is a perfect time to learn Surya Namaskar (literally, "sun greeting"). Surya Namaskar limbers up the whole body to prepare for the asana practice. This elegant series of twelve positions are performed as one continuous exercise. Each position of the salutation counteracts the one before, alternately contracting and expanding the chest in order to regulate breathing. Practicing Surya Namaskar daily (traditionally in the morning as a greeting to the sun) helps with overall flexibility as well as weight loss. By utilizing the previous month's yoga exercises in conjunction with Surya Namaskar, a regular beginning practice can begin to take shape. Start with four rounds a day and gradually build up from there.

SUN SALUTATIONS

1. Stand erect and bring the palms of your hands together in "namaste" in front of your chest. Exhale.

2. While inhaling, stretch your arms up and arch your back from the waist. Push your hips out with your legs remaining straight.

3. Exhale as you fold forward from the hips, pressing your palms down, and fingertips in line with your toes. Bend your knees if necessary.

4. Inhale as you step your left leg back and place your knee on the floor. Support your weight with your hands on the floor in a lunge position. Arch back and look up while lifting your chin.

5. Hold your breath as you bring the right leg back to align with your other leg behind you, forming a plank position. Keep your head and body in alignment and look between your hands.

6. On the exhale, lower your knees, then your chest and forehead to the ground while keeping your hips up and your toes curling under.

7. While inhaling, lower your hips to the floor, point your toes and arch your back. Keep your legs together and shoulders down. Fully extend your arms, look up, chin up.

8. Exhale and curl your toes under. Move into what is commonly known as Downward Dog. Raise your hips and pivot into an inverted "V" with your bottom in the air. Push your heels into the ground and keep your shoulders away from your ears while your head pushes down.

9. On the inhale, step forward and bring the right foot between your hands in a lunge position. Rest the other knee on the floor and look up.

10. While exhaling, bring the other leg forward to meet the first foot and bend over from the waist. Keep your palms beside each side, fingers pointing forward.

11. Inhaling, stand as you stretch your arms forward, then up and back over your head. Bend back slowly from your waist.

12. Exhale and gently come back to an upright position and bring your arms down to your sides.

Repeat all steps, this time using the opposite leg in steps 4-10. This is one round.

Chew on This

High levels of healthy fat is the preferred fuel of the human metabolism and has been proven to be key to health and peak brain function. Dietary habits for optimal brain health must include healthy fats on a daily basis. Healthy fats act as the vehicle that minerals, vitamins, and nutrients ride on to feed our brain what it needs to perform well.

Examples of healthy fats include:
- Plant-based: Organic avocado; organic extra virgin olive and organic coconut oil; nuts, excluding peanuts; and seeds from chia, flax, hemp, and pumpkin plants.
- Animal-based: Organic grass-fed and finished beef; pasture-raised chicken; wild-caught fish; organic grass-fed butter; and full-fat live culture yogurt.
- Supplements: MCT (medium-chain triglyceride) oil and fish oil, ensuring they are USDA organic, hexane free, and non-GMO.

QUICK HANDMADE GUACAMOLE

- 1 ripe avocado, cut in half, scooped, sliced, then mashed
- 1 small onion, minced
- 2 cloves of garlic, peeled and minced
- 1 small fresh tomato, seeded and diced
- 1 half lime, squeezed for juice
- *Optional, dice one small tomato

Place the mashed avocado in a bowl, add the onion, garlic, lemon juice and blend lightly leaving small chunks of avocado. Fold in the tomatoes just until blended. Serve with non-GMO crackers, organic pita bread, or tortilla chips.

Health Hint

Start your year right by minding your hydration levels. Yes, you hear it often, and now you're hearing it again. Drink half your weight in water every single day. Kick it up a notch by adding 1/8th of a teaspoon of Himalayan salt to every 20 ounces that you drink. The salt adds necessary trace minerals your body needs to be high functioning.

✵ www.TheEnergyAlmanac.com ✵

Notes

---◇◇◇---

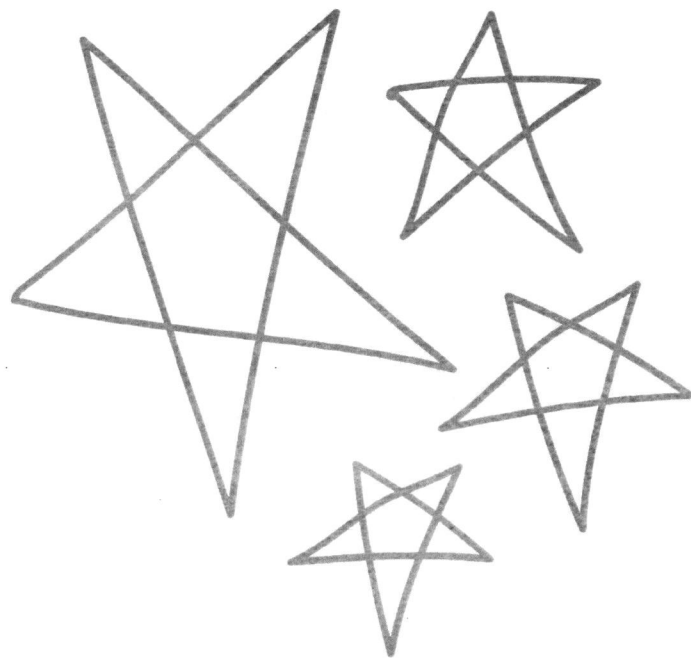

April

ACTIVITY, ENTHUSIASM, SHIFTS

APRIL 5-11

Do use restraint before deciding something.
Do not play victim if faced with setbacks.

APRIL 12-18

Do listen before leaping.
Do not move too fast.

APRIL 19-25

Do focus on loving and kind thoughts.
Do not be stubborn; you risk missing good guidance.

APRIL 26-30, MAY 1-2

Do seek balance between your own desires and the desires of others.
Do not be overly idealistic.

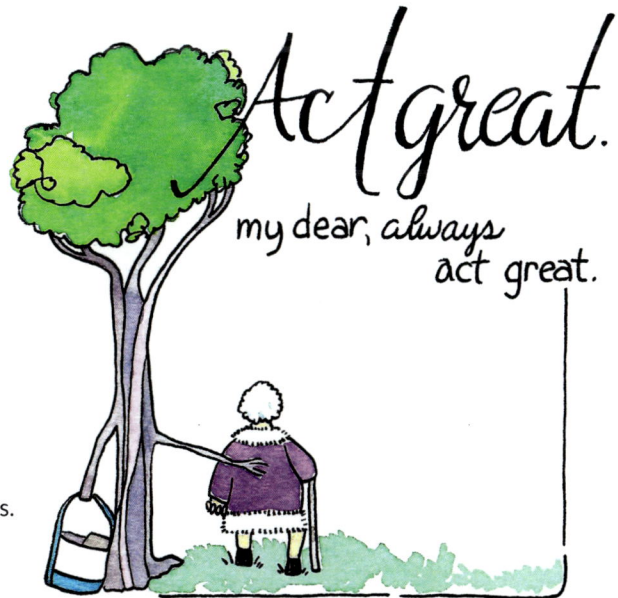

Act great. my dear, always act great.

WHAT IS POSSIBLE THAT I HAVEN'T EVEN CONSIDERED?

APRIL 11	APRIL 26
NEW MOON IN 22° ARIES	FULL MOON IN 7° SCORPIO
Be Fueled by Optimism	**Control or Conservation**

♡ Suns, Moons, and Success. Learn more: www.ChooseBigChange.com ♡

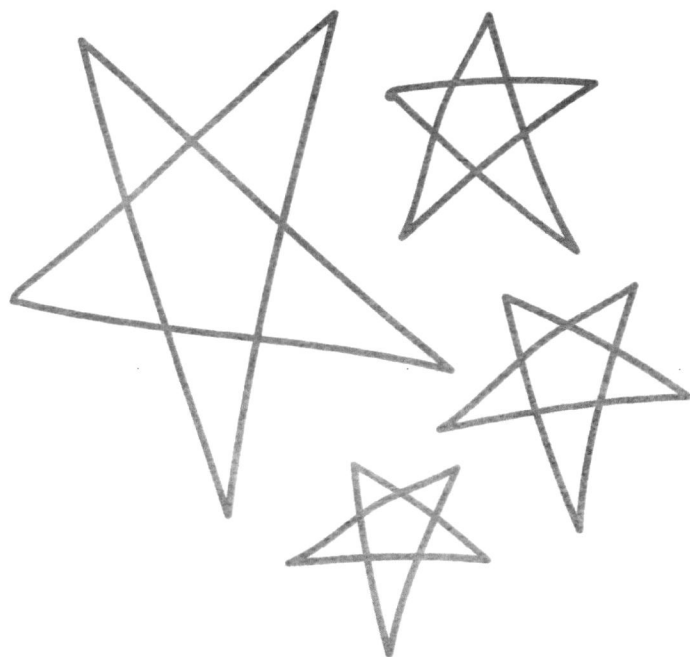

April

———— ◇◆◇ ————

Solar Cycle:
2ND QUARTER
Keywords:
ACTIVITY, ENTHUSIASM, SHIFTS

Early April's mix of air and fire planets fuels action, adventure, fun, communication, and progress. We're still in a waxing solar cycle with all planets in direct motion until the 27th. This is supportive for new beginnings and efforts to reach goals or complete projects. However, this month brings sign changes to all the inner planets, creating a variety of changes across the board that could indicate many personal shifts. After mid-month, planets moving through the conservative energy of Taurus could reawaken tensions between change and preservation. Uranus in Taurus (change and possessions) and Jupiter and Saturn in Aquarius (expansion, methods, and forward thinking) will be actively challenged. Notice as your emotions intensify near the Scorpio Full Moon on the 26th.

DATES TO WATCH:

- **April 4 Mercury enters Aries.** Quick thinking has pros and cons.

- **April 9 Mercury conjunct Chiron, Mars square Neptune.** Misunderstandings bring up old wounds.

- **April 11 Venus square Pluto.** Self-centered actions cause trouble with those in charge.

- **April 12 Aries New Moon.** *See April Moons section.*

- **April 14 Venus enters Taurus.** There will be stability in love and money.

- **April 16-17 Sun square Pluto, Mercury square Pluto.** Positive ideas and innovations face disapproval from someone in command.

- **April 19 Sun and Mercury enter Taurus.** Stability is in place. You are free to express yourself.

- **April 23 Mars enters Cancer.** Notice a passion for security and family.

- **April 26 Scorpio Full Moon.** *See April Moons section.*

- **April 29-30 Mercury sextile Neptune, Sun conjunct Uranus.** You may experience a shift of personal values near month's end.

♡ Suns, Moons, and Success. Learn more: www.ChooseBigChange.com ♡

APRIL ASTROLOGY BY THE WEEKS

APRIL 5-11

Lunar Signs:
CAPRICORN, AQUARIUS, PISCES, ARIES
Lunar Cycle:
4TH QUARTER

Mercury enters Aries bringing along fast thinking. Venus sextile Mars makes for a delightful relationship. Mars square Neptune, watch for irritation or confusion. Saturday Mercury sextile Saturn shepherds wise thinking, Venus sextile Jupiter allows for a happy gathering.

This week's energy is afloat with wisdom, new information, goodwill, and the beginning of a new cycle. Active, fiery thoughts and communication may require more restraint and consideration from you. Don't make a firm decision until you've seen all sides. Balance activity with some time to breathe and just relax, especially before sleep, or you risk a night of tossing and turning. Confusion and illusion are present this week but, when Saturday arrives, you will feel steady in your thoughts. Be ready for fun. Have an adventure with a group of friends where you can also learn exciting new things.

Shadow:
Don't let a setback create discouragement and doubt. Reaffirm goals and positive visions. Use silence to balance activity and you may receive important messages. Take a breath and ask "What's right about this setback that I can't see yet?"

APRIL 12-18

Lunar Signs:
ARIES, TAURUS, GEMINI, CANCER
Lunar Cycle:
NEW, 1ST QUARTER

Mercury sextile North Node and Aries New Moon is time to set intentions for action and new pathways. Pushing too hard may have consequences. This week's fast-paced enthusiasm may meet an obstacle.

If you received ideas last week, this week they may take form as you set your intentions at the Aries New Moon. Even as you sport the loveliest smile, however, you may hit a wall. If your enthusiasm about new ways puts off someone in authority who is guarding the status quo, you may need to adjust your course of action.

Venus shifting to steady Taurus on Wednesday brings a change in your love nature and what you value most. Part of you wants things to feel more grounded so you can quietly stop to smell the roses, but gee, it's an exciting time and things are going well. Try not to move too fast in a literal way or you could find yourself approaching the wrong person for approval. Those in charge may not be in alignment with new ideas. It's best to adhere to current regulations, no matter what thoughts and desires are propelling you forward. Hold off on your proposal to those in authority while you maintain your ideas and enthusiasm. You'll feel more grounded and focused on material matters soon enough. Right now, caution is needed to avoid negative consequences.

Shadow:
Failing to realize or acknowledge the power of current rules and regulations may have you pushing ahead enthusiastically without success. Stay open to realistic information which can reveal ways to adjust. Timing is everything.

APRIL 19-25

Lunar Signs:
CANCER, LEO, VIRGO, LIBRA
Lunar Cycle:
1ST QUARTER, 2ND QUARTER

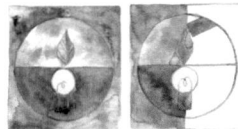

Friday Venus conjunct Uranus and Mars enters Cancer, creating a change in values and finance while stirring passion for security. Sunday Mercury square Saturn, Venus square Saturn, Mercury conjunct Venus means obstacles loom, but a heartfelt talk helps. This week holds the steady, peaceful energy of Sun, Mercury, and Venus in Taurus and the downshift in mental and outer activity.

Thoughts and activity begin to settle down to a steady pace as the week begins. Your enthusiasm may get squelched early on. Don't over-identify with your thoughts, especially if they hold rigid or stubborn opinions. A change in everyday matters can affect relationships and values nearer the weekend, but the remedy can be as simple as making changes in menus, home, or garden. Your desire to protect your home, family, and security grows as Mars enters Cancer.

Saturday can bring you a "eureka" moment. With it comes new information and communications that help you stay on track with your goals. Be aware that conflict arises Sunday between those who are more conservative and those with ideas about future potentials. If you focus your energy on loving thoughts and communication about the physical expression of life, nature, and the planet, things will lighten.

Shadow:
Don't let the Taurus attributes of stubbornness win. Soften yourself and see the value in a second point of view.

APRIL 26-30, MAY 1-2

Lunar Signs:
LIBRA, SCORPIO, SAGITTARIUS, CAPRICORN, AQUARIUS
Lunar Cycle:
FULL, 3RD QUARTER

Mercury sextile Neptune, Sun conjunct Uranus means a spiritual vision creates a major shift. There is a need for adjustment from last week's conflicts. The Scorpio Full Moon may assist.

At Monday's Full Moon you can seek to balance other people's values and requirements with your own. Review changes in your career, public life, and relationship to cultural values. Life will be flowing at a steady pace as the month of April ends. You should allow for psychic input to be balanced with practical thinking. This will create the ability to bring new practices into your financial life that may enrich how you experience the world in general. Notice how your own feelings of self-worth and gratitude are enhanced when you allow more spiritual and intuitive energy to lead the way.

You may receive a long-sought approval when Taurus Mercury trines Pluto, but don't become overly optimistic. Expect strong creative visions. Stay grounded to use this energy well and avoid getting lost in a lovely fantasy of romantic or creative conceptions. Schedule a brainstorm as successful talks and creative visions end this week.

Shadow:
Be wary of over-idealism. Stay practical. Ground your ideas with structure and order. Thorough planning will benefit you in the end.

♡ Suns, Moons, and Success. Learn more: www.ChooseBigChange.com ♡

April Moons

NEW MOON IN 22° ARIES ♈
APRIL 11, 2021 10:30 PM EDT

At this New Moon, set your intentions for the Aries areas of individuality, activity, adventure, and new beginnings. The Sun and Moon are joined with Venus, adding creative self-expression, feelings, love, and values to the mix. Despite the lowered energy of the New Moon phase, this planetary trio wants us to keep things moving. Can you feel the optimism? Let it fuel you.

The square to Pluto in Capricorn is the cog in the wheel this month and represents something in control (Pluto) that is resisting change(Capricorn). It is status quo versus forward flow. Consider where and how you want to move forward but feel held back by current rules and regulations. Watch for insights to arrive that light the way.

The night sky holds a square from Mars in Gemini to Neptune in Pisces. Be sure you don't have misinformation (Neptune) before you speak or act (Mars).

Pay attention to communication in your group interactions and with friends. Be mindful of how you communicate about your hopes and prospects. Remember, these thoughts are energy that will create that future.

_____

_____

_____

_____

FULL MOON IN 7° SCORPIO ♏
APRIL 26, 2021 11:31 PM EDT

The difference between the need for commitment, control, and sharing resources is now competing with your desire for personal finance, possessions, and preservation. This is the Moon in Scorpio opposite the Sun in Taurus.

There is a powerful fixed T-square formed as the Scorpio Moon and Taurus Sun both square Saturn in Aquarius. Tension is in the air. This conflict may focus on goals for the future. An objective mediator could help resolve any stalemates that arise, but there are planets linked against it that create remarkable resistance. Consider the values of other people. Share resources equitably or you risk relationships falling away.

Mars in Cancer, another aspect at play, will have you passionate about issues of home, family, and security. Enjoy domestic activities and joyful emotional interactions. A moonlight party might be just the right thing.

Your visions of the future should focus on expanding consciousness around marriage, women's rights, and ways to provide steady nourishment. Taurus loves food and beauty. What can you do to nourish your body and spirit?

_____

_____

_____

_____

Grab your free bonuses here: www.ChooseBigChange.com/bonus21

1 2 3 Numerology

A 9 month in a 5 year. Notice all the things in your life that you created and show gratitude for them. You are currently living with everything you have created. Embrace the present and be flexible enough to let go of the past. This month invites you to happy endings. This cycle symbolizes endings. Be mindful that endings bring new beginnings with it.

Gemstones

HOWLITE

Howlite is a serene white stone with veins of gray or brown. It is the stone of relief and calm. By activating the crown chakra, we gain perspective and feel more at ease. With the tendency to overdo activity and thinking this month, Howlite's calming energy and connection to higher energies inspire us to pause. It can also offer ease amid the stop and go by removing blocks. During times of expanding consciousness, Howlite effortlessly connects us to our wisdom and to receiving messages. This is an excellent stone for meditation. Be sure to use it daily to pause, rest, and calm your body and being. Harnessing the wind element, Howlite is amazing for promoting breathwork. It also offers clarity and movement.

Keywords: WISDOM, RELIEF, CALMING, AND RESTORATION.
Mantra: MY STILLNESS NOURISHES ME AND HEIGHTENS MY KNOWING.

Essential Oils

Who is up for action and adventure? April's planetary movement invites us to explore new beginnings with enthusiasm and propels us forward in reaching our goals. Tune into your intuition for clarity on which way to move.

FOR TOPICAL USE

Litsea: Apply 1-2 drops over the solar plexus and on the bottoms of your feet. This essential oil aids you in trusting your gut when deciding which ideas you want to follow through on. It assists in connecting you with your confidence and mobilizing your energy to move forward.

DIFFUSE THIS BLEND

- **Ginger 2 drops**
- **Wild Orange 3 drops**

Diffuse to be fully present and participate in life. Ginger is an empowering oil that supports us taking action. Wild Orange is a playful, uplifting oil to instill belief that you can accomplish your goals. This fun blend will give you a little pep in your step as you move throughout your day.

INGESTIBLE OPTIONS

Lime: The zest of life! Place 1-2 drops in your beverage. Its fresh taste is invigorating and adds enthusiasm and momentum.

♡ Suns, Moons, and Success. Learn more: www.ChooseBigChange.com ♡

VRIKSHASANA (TREE POSE)

vṛkṣāsana: vka:"tree"; *āsana*: "pose"

The ancients used the power of yoga to help them find inner and outer balance. Vrksasana (Sanskrit for "Tree Pose") is one such asana pose you can practice to find a calm center.

Yoga instructors will often combine the use of Trataka Gazing (see February's yoga) with Tree Pose, thus increasing the power of concentration and balance.

Physically, Tree Pose stretches the groin, thighs, torso and shoulders. It tones the abdominals, and increases strength and flexibility in the feet, ankles and calves. The pose can also help to correct flat feet and help reduce sciatica.

When life throws your footing off mentally or physically, Tree Pose can help you find your inner balance and calm concentration by muscle and mind retention. How can you use the lessons of Tree Pose in your daily life?

TREE POSE: "VRKSASANA" EXERCISE

1. Stand with your feet slightly closer together than shoulder width apart, arms relaxed at your sides. If comfortable, you may stand with feet together.

2. Take your attention to your feet. Feel your alignment strong and steady. Imagine that roots are reaching down from the soles of your feet deep into the earth, grounding or "rooting" you in place.

3. With soft eyes, find a point in front of you that is not moving to create one-pointed attention. Try not to let your eyes waver from this point.

4. Without looking away, turn your right foot out slightly to the right and slowly lift that leg until the knee is bent. Be aware of the rootedness of your left foot firmly on the ground.

5. Grab your right ankle with your right hand (if possible) and guide it so that the sole of your right foot is placed firmly on your inner left thigh, as close as possible to your groin. If you can't lift it that high, you may place the sole of your foot against the lower part of your inner left leg instead (such as just above your left ankle.) Do not place your foot against your knee.

6. Place your hands together in prayer position, "namaste", and breathe here for a moment. Don't be afraid to sway. Simply bring your attention back to your vision on the point ahead of you and to your left foot firmly on the ground.

7. When you're ready, you may bring your hands, still in prayer position toward the sky, fingertips pointing up. Breathe here with a natural, calm breath.

8. Without letting your eyes waver from your point of attention, return your right foot to the floor before repeating the routine on the other side with your left side.

9. When finished with both sides, stand with both feet on the ground and bring your arms gently down back to heart center, palms together.

10. Finish by bringing your hands back down to your sides and release your attention away from the point ahead of you.

Chew on This

As the earth starts to come alive with new growth, sprouts, and buds, we too can awaken our inner garden with the colors of spring. Eating foods from all colors of the spectrum encourage a diet that will nourish the mind and body and will enhance mental health. When we eat whole, nutrient-dense foods from the entire color spectrum, we obtain a mix of vitamins, minerals, and nutrients essential for health as each color brings different vitamins and healing nutrients for the body and the brain.

Be adventurous next time you're selecting your produce and "eat the rainbow"!

- **Red:** Red cabbage, red onions, red potatoes, radishes
  Benefits of Red: Improves memory, digestion, heart health, and lowers blood pressure

- **Orange:** Mangoes, oranges, butternut squash, nectarines, tangerines, carrots
  Benefits of Orange: Improves digestion, boosts immunity, prevents cellular damage, promotes healthy mucous membranes

- **Yellow:** Lemons, pineapple, yellow squash (delicata, acorn), yellow apples and pears
  Benefits of Yellow: Improves brain function, improves digestion, boosts immunity

- **Green:** Brussel sprouts, leeks, kale, lettuce, spinach, broccoli, green cabbage
  Benefits of Green: Detoxification, oxidative stress reduction, improves brain and liver function

- **Blue/Purple:** Purple kale, blackberries, plums, purple potatoes, purple grapes
  Benefits of Blue/Purple: Improves memory and circulation, boosts brain activity and immunity, improves digestion and blood sugar regulation

- **White:** Onions, garlic, cauliflower, Jerusalem artichoke, mushrooms
  Benefits of White: Reduces blood pressure, boosts immunity, lowers blood sugar, detoxification

Health Hint

Consider your vitamin D levels this month. Vitamin D is your friend as it enhances your immunity. With winter's shorter hours and reduced sunlight, adding some liquid vitamin D with K2 will amplify your body's capacity for healing. It strengthens the immune system, reducing the risk of auto-immune diseases.

♡ Suns, Moons, and Success. Learn more: www.ChooseBigChange.com ♡

Energy Almanac 2021 EDITION

Page 63

Notes

⸺ ◇◆◇ ⸺

_____
_____
_____
_____
_____
_____
_____
_____
_____
_____
_____
_____
_____
_____
_____
_____
_____
_____
_____
_____
_____
_____
_____
_____
_____

Grab your free bonuses here: www.ChooseBigChange.com/bonus21

May

COMMUNICATION, RELATIONSHIP, RETROGRADE

MAY 3-9

Do use your words and tone carefully.
Do not get stuck daydreaming.

MAY 10-16

Do notice the feeling of flow.
Do not fall prey to escapism.

MAY 17-23

Do get financial needs in order.
Do not skim the surface; seek additional information.

APRIL 26-30, MAY 1-2

Do expect some level of deception.
Do not stay caught up in fantasy.

Laugh BECAUSE THAT IS THE PUREST SOUND.

HOW CAN I PARTICIPATE MORE FULLY IN EASE?

MAY 11
NEW MOON IN 21° TAURUS
Material Matters

MAY 26
FULL MOON IN 5° SAGITTARIUS
Honesty & Truth Telling

Energy Almanac 2021 EDITION

♡ Suns, Moons, and Success. Learn more: www.ChooseBigChange.com ♡

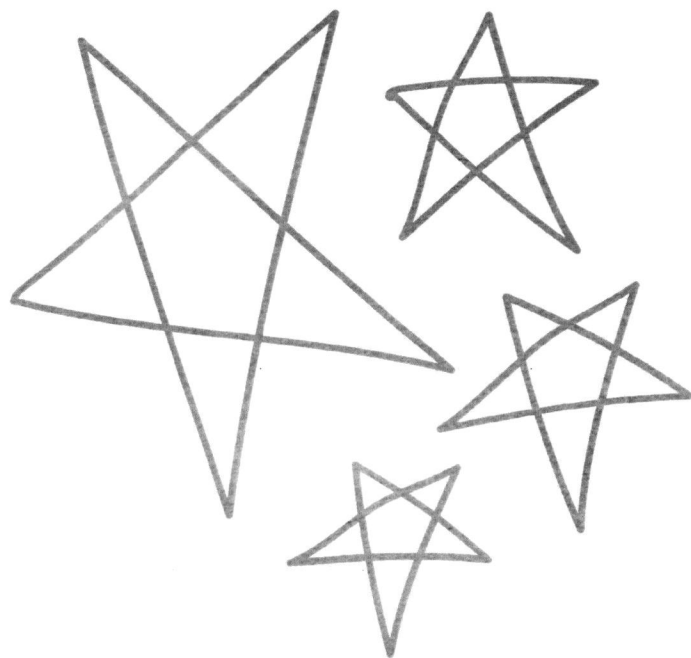

May

—◇◆◇—

Solar Cycle:
2ND QUARTER
Keywords:
COMMUNICATION, RELATIONSHIP, RETROGRADE

May is a gentle month in many ways. The major aspect is the Sagittarius Full Moon Lunar Eclipse coming at month's end which heightens your feelings and reveals relationship issues. Stay observant this month and communicate with the best possible outcome in mind. Use May for your personal enjoyment of reading, taking classes, and going on short journeys. You may be particularly drawn to areas featuring water. Later, when Jupiter moves into Pisces, you may feel more compassion and desire to aid those less fortunate. Expect intellectual activity and contact with siblings, family, and neighbors during May. With Mars in Cancer, you'll put some energy into securing your home, family, and comfort.

Saturn retrogrades in Aquarius on the 23rd. This begins the review of lessons learned in the areas of friendships, group affiliations, freedom, and goals for the future. Tension may rise between your solid shifts toward goals and surprising change in financial and geophysical events.

Mercury, planet of thinking and communication, slows down and retrogrades on May 29th. With this in mind, be sure to make major purchases and important decisions before the slowdown begins. Once Mercury is retrograde, anything beginning with 're' is supported (as in review, return, revisit, repair). Mercury goes direct again on June22nd.

DATES TO WATCH:

- **May 2-3 Venus sextile Neptune, Sun square Saturn, Mercury square Jupiter.** Romantic visions and overoptimism bump into sobering reality.

- **May 11 Taurus New Moon.** *See May Moons section.*

- **May 12 Mercury trine Saturn, Mars sextile Uranus.** Helpful meetings will bring good advice.

- **May 17-18 Sun trine Pluto, Venus conjunct North Node.** Pleasing communication during follow-up meetings brings those in charge on board with your plans.

- **May 21-23 Sun square Jupiter, Mercury square Neptune, Saturn retrogrades.** Overoptimism, overdoing, and misinformation threaten your recent gains.

- **May 26 Sagittarius Full Moon Lunar Eclipse.** Feelings and relationship issues come to a peak. Something can no longer be ignored. *See May Moons section.*

- **May 29 Mercury conjunct Venus, Mercury retrogrades.** Promises are sweet, but your mind can and will change in the future.

♡ Suns, Moons, and Success. Learn more: www.ChooseBigChange.com ♡

MAY ASTROLOGY BY THE WEEKS

MAY 3–9	**Lunar Signs:** AQUARIUS, PISCES, ARIES, TAURUS **Lunar Cycle:** 3RD TO 4TH QUARTER

Mercury square Jupiter, Sun square Jupiter combine highs and lows. A shift in thoughts when Mercury enters Gemini. Venus trine Pluto creates powerful romantic and/or business encounters. Venus square Jupiter, begs you to watch for overindulgence. Venus enters Gemini, offering loving words.

Your plans may be derailed by obstacles this week. Don't let it lower your confidence. A shift in perspective comes as you emphasize gathering information and new ideas and making new contacts. Things take a turn for the better when you implement solid advice from a trusted advisor. Work to stay on course and reach your goal. Leave space in your calendar for a fated meeting in love or business. You may be tempted to overdo spending or other pleasures over the weekend. You'll be in a new, lighthearted frame of mind once Venus enters Gemini. This is a positive energy for communication and networking; use it in that way. With Venus in this sign, remember *how* you say it is as important as *what* you're saying. A spoonful of sugar truly makes the medicine go down and makes people more willing to listen to what you have to say.

Shadow:
Daydreams can be dangerous. Positive vision that leads to manifestation differs from fanciful imagination. One is aligned with purpose while the other weakens your power.

MAY 10–16	**Lunar Signs:** TAURUS, GEMINI, CANCER **Lunar Cycle:** 4TH QUARTER, NEW, 1ST QUARTER

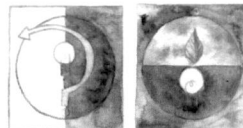

Lower energy and a focus on things to release will precede the Taurus New Moon; set your intentions on material matters. Mars sextile Uranus, Mercury trine Saturn, be ready to begin new projects in practical ways. Sun sextiles Neptune and Jupiter enters Pisces, shifts into a gentle-feelings mode.

Here's a week where all elements combine to make things flow easily. You've got ideas about what you want to manifest in the area of finance, possessions, real estate, and home. You're ready to take positive action to secure your needs and make wise plans for the future.

A dreamier mode comes after this, when you can receive intuitive guidance and enjoy creative projects and entertainment. You will feel the stirrings of expansion in the sign of spirituality, arts, music, and dance. Plan a course of action to eliminate escapist behaviors, addictions, and feelings of martyrdom during the transit of Jupiter in Pisces that starts this week.

Shadow:
Watch your desire for instant gratification. Maintain common sense, practice patience, and get fulfillment through a gratitude practice. Good things come to those who wait.

MAY 17-23

Lunar Signs:
CANCER, LEO, VIRGO, LIBRA, SCORPIO
Lunar Cycle:
1ST QUARTER, 2ND QUARTER

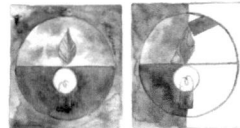

Sun trine Pluto, Venus conjunct North Node means progress toward goals and helpful information. Venus trines Saturn, Sun enters Gemini for positive connections with friends and extra energy in the mind and on the subject of relations. The Sun squares Jupiter for logic flooded by feelings. Mercury square Neptune brings misinterpretations and confusion.

With the Sun still in Taurus as the week begins, you may find yourself enjoying time in nature or sharing wonderful food with loved ones. Mercury is getting closer to slowing down before its retrograde, so take advantage of Monday's opportunity to get financial and career needs under control. Nurture the growth of your goals by communicating with those who can provide solid advice for the future. (Do you have a mentor yet?) Review any aspects of career or goals to see what systems need to be tweaked for greater success. Check your timing! Stay conscious of your true needs when the urge to overdo and over-expand show up. Near the end of the week, communications are confusing and could well be deceptive, so stay alert.

Shadow:
Be sure to fact check before you act on important matters. Don't just skim the surface. Stay grounded in reality.

MAY 24-30

Lunar Signs:
LIBRA TO CAPRICORN
Lunar Cycle:
2ND QUARTER, FULL, 3RD QUARTER

The Sagittarius Full Moon Lunar Eclipse, Venus square Neptune has the world exploring vision versus fantasy. Mercury retrograde and conjunct Venus means promises can change.

You may be feeling increasingly frustrated by a lack of clarity. For relief, make a decision and stick to it. But do be mindful that things may look better than they really are. As you begin to review all the thoughts, decisions, and conversations from the past month, you may see them in a different light. Look through the lens of peaceful resolutions.

This week, as Mercury slows down to station retrograde, communications are confusing or deceptive. Even Siri has bad days, or a GPS gives wrong directions. Don't allow fear to overcome your better judgment and positive inner direction. The Lunar Eclipse brings all feelings to a peak and can shed light on areas where common perspectives and beliefs are absent. While Mercury stations retrograde, there is a potential for reconciliation and words of love to be exchanged. Discover if promises and sweet words are something you can truly count on or deliver. Mercury retrograde in Gemini is best used for reviewing the previous weeks and any relationship issues. You can also continue with projects begun before the middle of the month.

Shadow:
Fantasy can lead to let down. Getting caught up in beautiful dreams and believing false communications leads you astray. Be realistic about how you proceed.

♡ Suns, Moons, and Success. Learn more: www.ChooseBigChange.com ♡

Energy Almanac 2021 Edition

Page 69

May Moons

NEW MOON IN 21° TAURUS
MAY 11, 2021 2:59 PM EDT

Set your intentions for the Taurus areas of finance, real estate, garden, possessions, values, and self-worth. What would please you the most? More money? A spectacular new sofa? Feeling more confident?

If you look around, you'll see someone who is established offering help, and you will have lovely creative impulses. Be careful, these impulses can be offset by a tendency to be overly optimistic or overindulgent. Apply clear thinking as you set intentions for future goals and be ready to implement changes that will enhance your sense of security. A general sense of imbalance, both in our personal lives and the outer world, comes from planets that are clustered in only one half of the zodiac. A lack of fire planets combined with the naturally occurring lower energy at any New Moon may bring lethargy and lack of initiative to take action toward goals. Don't let this discourage you. Stay aligned with your own vision. This too shall pass.

FULL MOON IN 5° SAGITTARIUS (LUNAR ECLIPSE)
MAY 26, 2020 11:13 AM EDT

This Full Moon brings emphasis to the differences between the need for expansive philosophical views (go Sag!) and the expression of logical, detailed information (Gemini). Remember, every Full Moon is an opposition to the Sun. The Sun is currently in Gemini, the Moon is, of course, in Sagittarius.

Work to find common ground and you will see that communication and cooperation can be achieved. A Full Moon that is also a Lunar Eclipse brings relationship differences to a peak and a shift will take place at some point during the next six months. Sagittarian spiritual perspectives and guidance hold the key to resolving the differences you have. Be aware! Pleasant thoughts and spoken words that won't hold water ultimately disappoint.

You may have creative ideas around change for the future. Watch for difficulty between those ideals and an authoritarian with power. He/she may desire the status quo or a different timeline. Honesty is the key to understanding what is possible and what is not. Once you find and express this truth, a solution with the most beneficial outcome can be found and everyone can rest easy.

Grab your free bonuses here: www.ChooseBigChange.com/bonus21

1 2 3 Numerology

A 1 month in a 5 year. This is a month for new starts. It's time for you to stand on your own and make decisions. Be precise and definite about your desired outcome when making choices. After you set your intentions, use this month's energy of new possibilities to intuitively provide clarity to those intentions. How you feel about your life will be revealed to you through circumstances. Be open to the universe putting you in a special position that may initiate a new life.

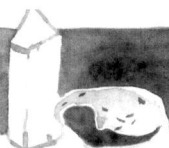

Gemstones

BANDED AGATE

Banded Agate is a subtle stone containing gentle bands of white and gray. It is a healing stone for body, mind, and spirit. Agates tend to cleanse and balance all chakras, but this agate also activates the root chakra. With Mars in Cancer, Banded Agate nourishes your desire for security, home life, comfort, and nourishment. It will also enhance your focus at a time of overthinking and support your health despite the pull of instant gratification. With Banded Agate encouraging balance and clarity, we can attain ease with communication and confusion. Use this stone during meditation to cleanse and balance all of your chakras. Harnessing the water element, Banded Agate is great for releasing what is no longer serving you and calling in clarity with stillness.

Keywords: CALM, GOOD LUCK, WEALTH, HEALTH, STABILITY, BALANCE, AND FOCUS
Mantra: MY BODY, MIND, AND SPIRIT ARE CLEAR AND BALANCED.

Essential Oils

We enter this month with the theme of communication and review. With an uptick in the receiving of thoughts and information, you are given the opportunity to learn. We are also being asked to review lessons learned as we enter into Mercury Retrograde at the end of the month. Special attention to focus will be helpful at this time. You may also find great benefit and support in your rituals, practices, and routines. Work with the oils selected to help you navigate your way.

FOR TOPICAL USE

Spearmint: Place 1-2 drops over the throat or on bottoms of feet. An uplifting oil that stimulates clarity of thought, Spearmint also creates confident communication.

DIFFUSE THIS BLEND

- **Tangerine 3 drops**
- **Peppermint 2 drops**
- **Lavender 1 drop**

The suggested blend of Tangerine, Peppermint, and Lavender will support you creatively and energize you as it helps you focus, and it will support your communication needs.

INGESTIBLE OPTIONS

Lemon: This delightful and popular oil will aid and support you with focus. It helps you to be mentally present and fills the body, mind, and soul with energy, alertness, and confidence. Take 1-2 drops under the tongue or in a beverage. Add to your favorite white cake batter or a fresh batch of white rice to add little zing.

♡ Suns, Moons, and Success. Learn more: www.ChooseBigChange.com ♡

Energy Almanac 2021 EDITION

Page 71

NAVASANA: BOAT POSE
Navasana: nava: boat. *āsana:* posture

Our hips and abdomen are what help us lift our bodies up and move. We use these muscles 24 hours a day, even in sleep while we breathe deep, and yet, focusing on strengthening our core is so often neglected. This leads to weakening over time. You can help strengthen your hip flexors and abdomen by practicing yoga poses specifically made to target those areas. Navasana, or Boat Pose, is one such pose.

Joe Pilates first taught his system of core strengthening to dancers and performers of the early 19th century. Boat Pose quickly became the poster child of the Pilates system for its ability to strengthen the hips, thighs, and abdomen and to help create power and the strong uplift needed in performance. Another benefit of Boat Pose is its proficiency in strengthening the lungs; through the intense upward motion of the legs, chest and arms, air is forcibly pushed into and out of the lungs thereby strengthening and toning them.

BOAT POSE

Boat Pose can be demanding. If you feel strain in your back, relax and start again. In time, your core muscles will become stronger, allowing you to perform the pose through to completion and repetition. Remember to keep your breath even and your jaw soft during this pose. It is recommended to repeat the pose three times.

1. Start in a seated position with knees bent and tip of toes on the floor.
2. Bring your fingertips to touch the floor behind you for support.
3. Engage your abdominal muscles as you slowly lean back with the support of your fingertips.
4. Lift feet until shins are parallel to the floor.
5. Keeping knees bent, draw your thighs close to your chest and lift your chest toward your thighs. Keep your head level and your vision just over and beyond the tips of your toes.
6. Gently squeeze your thighs together.
7. To release the pose, slowly bend the knees, release your feet to the floor.

Chew on This

Our body is made up of between 60-75% water. It's no surprise that how much (or how little) you drink can affect your health. Too much water could result in mineral imbalances while too little could cause dehydration, headaches, poor complexion, tight muscles, and fatigue. So, how much should you drink? Water intake does vary from male to female and varies with each individual's lifestyle and diet. On average, men should ingest about 3 liters (13 cups) and women about 2.2 liters (9 cups) of water each day. *(This is approximately half your weight in ounces of water.)* In order to satisfy individual needs, various lifestyle factors need to be taken into consideration. For example, the water content in fresh fruits and green leafy vegetables may increase hydration in the body, but if the same person exercises and sweats on a daily basis, more water may need to be consumed.

Benefits of drinking water:

- **Boosts metabolism and turns on your internal incinerator.** Before you even go to the bathroom, chug water upon rising in the morning. This jump starts your metabolism out of the gate. Not to mention, we wake up dehydrated from not having drunk a drop all night while sleeping.

- **Promotes digestion.** Water is a vehicle to deliver nutrients throughout the body and encourages circulation.

- **Detox your body.** Have healthier skin and more energy. Drink up to boost your body's natural detoxification process and flush out those toxins. Hydration improves complexion, energy and focus.

- **Decrease hunger and manage your weight.** Not drinking enough water is a major reason for increased hunger and decreased satiety and cravings.

Don't enjoy plain water? Add fresh herbs, cucumber slices, or lemons slices (or a combination of all of these) to a jug of water and keep it in your refrigerator. For added fun and to help you commit to drinking it, call it your "spa water".

Health Hint

Did you know that vitamin C is the most widely known immune-boosting micronutrient? It stimulates white blood cells in your body to help prevent disease. Eating oranges most likely isn't providing you enough. Liquid Liposomal vitamin C is excellent supplementation. A minimum of 2500 IU's daily is a standard maintenance dose for most people.

♡ Suns, Moons, and Success. Learn more: www.ChooseBigChange.com ♡

Page 73

Notes

—◇❖◇—

Grab your free bonuses here: www.ChooseBigChange.com/bonus21

✫ www.TheEnergyAlmanac.com ✫

June

FAMILY, CREATIVITY, REVIEW

MAY 31, JUNE 1-6

Do notice a wave of hope and optimism.
Do not avoid warning signs.

JUNE 7-13

Do set intentions around family and everyday environment.
Do not avoid reviewing your past six months.

JUNE 14-20

Do slow down to avoid making mistakes.
Do not be complacent.

JUNE 21-27

Do be willing to see things differently.
Do not hold on to old ideas for too long.

JUNE 28-30, JULY 1-4

Do enjoy pleasant times with family.
Do not push forward at this time.

Be WITH THOSE WHO HELP YOUR being

WHAT ARE THE GREATEST POSSIBILITIES AVAILABLE NOW?

JUNE 10

NEW MOON IN 19° GEMINI

Seeking Higher Vision

JUNE 24

FULL MOON IN 3° CAPRICORN

Exploring Home and Work

♡ Suns, Moons, and Success. Learn more: www.ChooseBigChange.com ♡

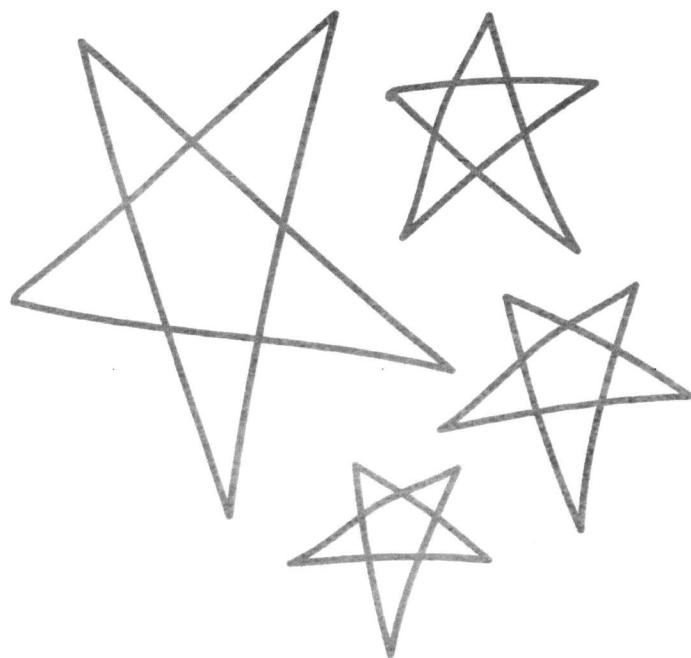

June

—◇◈◇—

Solar Cycle:
2ND QUARTER, FULL, 3RD QUARTER
Keywords:
FAMILY, CREATIVITY, REVIEW

In June, the Sun's rays carry the Gemini influence into your creative self-expression until it enters Cancer at the Summer Solstice on the 20th. It covers the area of family, neighbors, local travel, and everyday environments.

Mercury continues in Gemini this month and stays retrograde until the 22nd. A Solar Eclipse takes place at the Gemini New Moon on June 10th. Change and a new beginning will occur, both personally and collectively, over the next six months.

Sensitivity, sentimentality, and feelings of love for home and family will increase, along with a desire to nurture as we move into the Cancer influence. You may notice that your own desire for security increases. Mars will enter Leo just after the Solar Eclipse, bringing action and passion to romance, parenting, creativity and investment. Surprises could undo plans that were already in place. A review of strategy, systems, and timing for future goals is required this month. On the day with the longest hours of light, Summer Solstice coincides with the Sun's entry into Cancer on the 20th. The Sun in Cancer amplifies sensitivity and focus on family while the retrograde of Jupiter means that in general, benefits slow down. Neptune is retrograde too. Phew! Expect intuitive, artistic, and spiritual energy to be more internalized.

It's time to examine the fruition of the last six months. Acknowledge your achievements and share some of the bounty with others. There is more affection, drama, loyalty and love available at month's end. You'll see it in the form of self-expression, creativity, entertainment, parenting, romance, and investment. With both Mars and Venus in Leo now, the last four days of June are perfect for weddings, parties, and beach vacations in the sun. Plan something fun.

DATES TO WATCH:

- **June 2-3 Sun trine Saturn, Venus trine Jupiter.** Stable thoughts and planning combine with feelings of optimism and gratitude.

- **June 5 Mercury square Neptune, Mars opposes Pluto.** Signals are crossed. Security and protection issues clash with a power figure. Confusion clashes with anger and there may be some impulsive actions.

- **June 10 Gemini New Moon Solar Eclipse.** *See June Moons section.*

- **June 13-14 Sun square Neptune, Venus sextile Uranus, Saturn square Uranus.** Confusion combines with a desire to find secure ways to approach shifting values. Meanwhile, another surprising shift arrives.

- **June 20 Summer Solstice.** The waxing solar cycle peaks on the day with the longest hours of light.

- **June 22-24 Mercury stations direct.** Communications begin to clear up.

- **June 24, Full Moon in Capricorn.** *See June Moons section.*

♡ Suns, Moons, and Success. Learn more: www.ChooseBigChange.com ♡

Energy Almanac 2021 EDITION

Page 77

JUNE ASTROLOGY BY THE WEEKS

MAY 31, JUNE 1-6

Lunar Signs:
AQUARIUS, PISCES, ARIES, TAURUS
Lunar Cycle:
3RD QUARTER, 4TH QUARTER

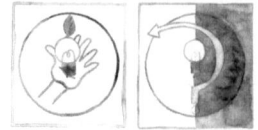

Mars trines Neptune, bringing ideals about home and family. Sun joins the Gemini North Node and Venus enters Cancer, bringing greater focus on thoughts and communication about love of home and family. Sun trines Saturn and Venus trines Jupiter, bringing along a festive mood and optimistic thoughts. Mercury squares Neptune and Mars opposes Pluto; watch for confusion and conflict.

You may have the desire and ability to take positive actions and secure situations with your home and family on Monday. You could even have an 'aha' moment. Your sudden insight, along with love for family and other special ones, goes a long way toward improving relationships. On Thursday, gather with friends, have optimism, and share goodwill as you give and receive support for future plans.

Troubling conditions arrive on Saturday when communications are confusing. You could experience an angry confrontation between someone passionate about home and family and someone else obsessed with power. As we all move closer to the New Moon Eclipse, this interaction can help you see something that needs to be released.

Shadow:
Be mindful of wanting to plunge ahead despite signals to retreat. It's time to ponder and intuit any changes ahead before the Solar Eclipse New Moon arrives next week.

JUNE 7-13

Lunar Signs:
TAURUS, GEMINI, CANCER, LEO
Lunar Cycle:
4TH QUARTER, NEW, 1ST QUARTER

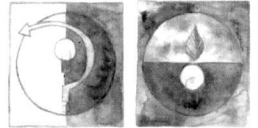

Gemini New Moon Eclipse arrives; set intentions. Sun joins Mercury, Mars enters Leo, thoughts are active, passion and pride combine. Venus sextile Uranus brings positive change. Sun squares Neptune and suddenly self-expression blurs.

A quiet beginning to this week will give you time to focus on intentions for the New Moon. As momentum accelerates, you experience passion and a value for practical change. Stay alert because confusing information and surprising change can force you to shift directions.

Approaching the eclipsed New Moon, you have time to review and see what might be changing in the next six months. This is surely regarding your outer life. Set Gemini New Moon intentions concerning the areas of study, short journeys, siblings and family, neighborhood, and everyday environments. Where have you noticed change, and what improvement needs to be made next? Think back. Remember conversations and thoughts of the past few weeks. Do you see things differently now or have a better idea of how to communicate your needs? Surprising changes over the weekend may involve food or real estate and seem easy to accommodate, but there is confusion over directions, and nobody knows who is in charge. Make sure you're not taking on more than you should, and for goodness sake, don't leave situations in the wrong hands.

Shadow:
Choosing to be in denial about your part of the problem won't help. Notice and admit to missteps and practice patience with yourself for the learning curve you're on.

JUNE 14-20

Lunar Signs:
LEO, VIRGO, LIBRA, SCORPIO
Lunar Cycle:
1ST QUARTER, 2ND QUARTER

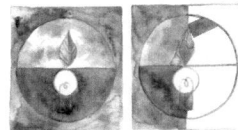

Exact Saturn Uranus square means future plans and changes bring conflict. The absence of planetary aspects from Tuesday through Sunday allows time for assimilating and contemplating information. Mercury slows down to station for direct motion, encouraging a review of the past. The Sun enters Cancer at the Summer Solstice on the 20th (EDT), ending the 2021 waxing solar cycle.

The week starts out rough. There is conflict between your strategies (Saturn) and a sudden shift (Uranus) that might disrupt current foundations. It's a good time to review plans and set your intentions for positive outcomes.

This is the last week of Mercury's retrograde in Gemini. Use this time to process and review the past six months and more recent events. Be aware of the coming week's Mercury station on the 21st. When Mercury stations, it's as though the mind stands still and you (and others) are more prone to making mistakes.

On the Summer Solstice, find a way to celebrate your achievements over the past six months. Cultivate the momentum needed to continue through the waning solar cycle (the time when the sun's light begins to decrease). Find ways to express gratitude to those who've supported your efforts and begin to share the fruits of your experience and successes with others.

Shadow:
Be mindful of complacency. You must be able to respond thoughtfully when shifts occur. A thorough review will benefit you. Don't pass up the opportunity to be flexible now.

JUNE 21-27

Lunar Signs:
SAGITTARIUS, CAPRICORN
Lunar Cycle:
2ND QUARTER

Venus trines Neptune, bringing creative and romantic visions. Mercury goes direct, allowing for clarity of thought. Feelings intensify for the Capricorn Full Moon on the 24th; there could be a serious disagreement to handle. Mars sextiles North Node, passion pursues information. Venus enters Leo where romance and creativity are valued.

This is a week of highs and lows that ends with a sense of better things to come.

Use an expanded level of compassion and optimism to deal with any conflicts between love of domesticity versus a powerful focus on public life. The Capricorn Full Moon is bringing this to the surface. Now is a good time to consider the effects of thoughts and words combined with detailed information to guide your desire for creative self-expression. As Mercury resumes direct motion in Gemini, you will begin to see things differently. Discard some previous ideas and see what you can discover that is more appealing. It's best to wait and let more be revealed during the coming week. Don't act on important matters just yet.

Shadow:
Don't hold on to old ideas for too long. Space and time allow for an improved way forward. Be willing to let that new idea in.

♡ Suns, Moons, and Success. Learn more: www.ChooseBigChange.com ♡

Page 79

JUNE 28-30, JULY 1-4

Lunar Signs:
AQUARIUS, PISCES
Lunar Cycle:
3RD QUARTER

The last three days of June have no planetary aspects, so your thoughts and activities can drift in pleasant waters. Mars opposes Saturn on Thursday, bringing along conflict. Mars square Uranus, Venus sextile North Node, watch as tensions erupt but kind words soothe. The 4th of July can be volatile. Caution is needed.

Late June offers us an opportunity to relax and ponder how our thoughts have changed during the Mercury retrograde. What is it that you want to change or pursue? It's still not time to push forward with important purchases or new projects. All outer planets except Uranus are now in retrograde which brings a noticeable downshift in many areas of life. Instead of resisting, spend time looking over life areas to see what has been attained and what can still be gained. A deep dive is in order. Journal or communicate what you've learned and begin to examine yourself for ways you've changed over the first half of 2020.

Spend time in creative activities. Enjoy trips, parties, entertainment, time with children, and sharing affection with a special someone.

As July begins, thunderstorms of discontent and discord begin to form. Passions are strong and need to be tempered with wisdom.

The quiet peace at the end of June shifts dramatically in early July as strong feelings about loved ones and personal expression are faced with the demands of a larger group. You should seek information and the right words to help calm the situation.

Shadow:
Don't push. In all things, timing matters. With a multitude of outer planets retrograde, now is the time for review and reflection rather than aggressive action for the sake of forward movement.

June Moons

NEW MOON (SOLAR ECLIPSE) IN 19° GEMINI
JUNE 10, 2021 6:52 AM EDT

When the Gemini New Moon Eclipse arrives, you should set intentions for communication, study, short journeys, siblings, family, neighbors, and local or everyday surroundings. Mars takes a final, passionate stand for home, family, and security under this moon, but with the Sun, Moon and retrograde Mercury square Neptune in Pisces, your thoughts may become clouded. This leads to some misleading information. If you can hold a higher vision it may solve any discrepancy in beliefs, thoughts, and perceptions and help handle the coming conflicts. Stable structures will once again be challenged by a force that desires change. The Cancer traits of love and value for home, family, and nurturing will work with changes to maintain security. Do hold a vision of transformation in the outer world to get the best possible results for everyone involved.

Everyone will have a change in one area of their outer world. If you know your natal (birth) chart, seek the house where this Solar Eclipse falls, and you'll discover in which area of life the change will occur. *(Schedule a natal chart reading with your favorite astrologer. Ours is Shellie Enteen. Her bio is in the resource section.)*

_____
_____
_____

FULL MOON IN 3° CAPRICORN
JUNE 24, 2021 2:39 PM EDT

This Full Moon activates the polarity between the need for public life, career, and achievement (Capricorn) versus expressing yourself in the areas of security, home, family, and nurturing (Cancer). Since this Full Moon is the opposite to the Cancer Full Moon Eclipse that happened in January, it's the perfect time to ask yourself what changes have occurred in your relationships since then. Explore how you are handling work and social needs and home life now. You may see challenges in both investments and in building foundations for the future while handling actual shifts in finance.

Devotion to a spiritual practice for guidance and surrender can be the ointment for the wound. Be mindful that any spiritual focus will be challenged by Mercury in Gemini conjunct North Node which seeks information and wants to logically analyze everything. Trust that this spiritual practice is the way to find peace now.

23 Numerology

A 2 month in a 5 year. Events may surface that challenge you into taking swift quick, decisive action. You are being surrounded by excitement and stimulation. Stay focused on your intentions and goals so you aren't being driven by impulses. Strategize what you can do now that you haven't done before to create a new desired outcome. This could be the month to settle any partnership complications.

Gemstones

TURQUOISE

Turquoise is an eye-catching stone of greenish-blue color. It is believed to be one of the oldest used stones and has a rich history in many cultures and countries. Turquoise activates and cultivates spiritual expansion and activates the throat chakra. With the New Moon Eclipse, it is the perfect moment for spiritual expansion by releasing limiting beliefs, mental burdens, fears, and failures. We are also drawn to gather this month, and Turquoise brings us ease with communication and awareness of our heart space. It encourages us to break free of being the savior and find enlightenment through self-kindness. Turquoise is great for meditation and for allowing our being to expand beyond this reality. It harnesses the storm element which includes the aspects of wind, water, earth and fire simultaneously. This makes it a powerhouse and brings freedom from fear and limitation.

Keywords: COMMUNICATION, SPIRITUAL EXPANSION, ENLIGHTENMENT AND WHOLENESS.
Mantra: I EXPAND INTO THE WHOLENESS OF THE UNIVERSE AND MY DEEPEST WISDOM.

Essential Oils

As we start off the month with Mercury Retrograde, be patient. It may take some time for the fog to clear. There is a strong focus on coming together this month. It is a good time for gatherings of family and friends. During this time, we are asked to reflect on how far we've come, what we have accomplished, and to celebrate this with others. In the essence of sharing and showing love to those dear to us during gatherings and to ignite the spirit of playfulness, use these oils to lovingly support you.

FOR TOPICAL USE

Ylang Ylang: Apply 1-2 drops over the heart or to the bottom of feet. Ylang Ylang reconnects us with our inner child. It helps us see and appreciate all the beautiful blessings in life.

Clary Sage: Apply 1-2 drops to the forehead. Clary sage aids in removing creative blocks.

DIFFUSE THIS BLEND

- **Grapefruit 3 drops**
- **Spearmint 4 drops**
- **Bergamot 3 drops**
- **Hawaiian Sandalwood: 2 drops**

When diffused, this combination supports decision making, strength and certainty, optimism, love, and compassion, making it a compelling blend to use often during a month when gathering together is urged.

INGESTIBLE OPTIONS

Red Mandarin: A sweet citrus that invites you to appreciate the sweetness of life, Red Mandarin encourages all to remember the playful innocence of childhood. It also helps the tired parent refocus on the magic of life's simple moments. This lovely oil will also evoke feelings of safety. Take 1-2 drops under the tongue or in a beverage.

UTKATASANA : CHAIR POSE
Utkaṭasana: utkata: wild, intense. _āsana:_ posture, seat

In more challenging yoga poses, such as the deceptively intense Utkatasana, or Chair Pose, there is an opportunity to stay calm and focused through the pose by using deep yogic breathing. Practicing such difficult poses conditions our bodies and minds to stay calm during difficult times off the mat and in our daily lives.

With Chair Pose, the asana is simple in action, but the mind of the beginning yogi tends to wander in moments of intensity with each passing second of the pose. Utkata has several meanings such as: intense, wild, and frightening. These very things in life present us with the most opportunity for growth. With practice, you can utilize the true outcome of Chair Pose: that of becoming courageous in the face of adversity. With a bit of practice and patience, you can conquer this pose.

Chair Pose conditions the legs, back, and arms. It also gives awareness to how our hip flexors, knees, and ankles flex and perform in our daily lives and the relationship between your hips and lower back. The knees bend, engaging the thigh muscles (rectus femoris) and the hip flexor muscles (iliopsoas). These muscles working together allows you to go into deep squats and stabilize the pelvis.

CHAIR POSE

With this pose, deep yogic breathing (pranayama) is useful to gather your inner and outer strength and go deeper into the pose. We recommend you revisit January's yoga entry on pranayama and practice Ujjai breathing with this pose. It is also important to keep a relaxed jaw and soft eyes throughout the pose. It is recommended that you hold the pose for three breaths and repeat the pose up to three times.

1. Begin by standing in Tadasana (Standing Pose) with your big toes touching and the outside edge of your feet parallel with one another. Back is straight, chin level with the ground, your vision is straight ahead. Arms at your sides.

2. Place your hands on your hips, bend your knees and lower your hips as if you are sitting down onto a chair. Keep both knees facing forward.

3. Push down through your heels as if rooting them down into the earth. Lower as far as you can until you are at a maximum without strain.

4. Lengthen your tailbone down toward the ground and draw up through your hips and lower abdomen in order to create length in your lower back as you lift your chest. Watch out for any tilting forward of your pelvis and remedy this by curling your tailbone further under and down. If you feel any strain in your back, lift out of the pose slightly and tuck your tailbone down even more strongly in order to create more strength and balance in your hips and back.

5. Bring your palms together and feel your shoulder blades draw in. Broaden your collarbones and lift your chest a little more.

6. With calm but strong breath, reach your arms up, shoulder width apart and palms facing each other. Your inner biceps should be facing your ears.

7. Gather your power through your rooted feet and strong breath, as you lengthen up through the outer ribs, through your inner arms, and all the way up to the tips of your fingers.

8. To release the pose, straighten your legs and release your arms to your sides.

Chew on This

As we invite summer in this month, we start to see an increase in social activities. Friends and family are joining together for barbeques, dips in the pools, trips to the beach, hikes in woods, and an increased sense of community overall. As we deepen our connection with others around us, we can also deepen our connection with our local food. For most areas, June is abundant with local produce, honey, eggs, herbs and more!

For centuries we hunted, grew, and foraged our food in our immediate surroundings. Fortunately, sourcing food today isn't quite so challenging, but eating foods grown by our local farmers is a smart choice in many ways. Produce bought from local farms is typically organic (double check with your local farmer). Eating organic versus genetically modified organisms (GMO's) ensures a healthier gut flora. Organic farming is also the best form of farming for our environment, making sure no chemicals go into the ground or our streams, rivers, and other water sources. When we shop at a local farmers' market, we inject our money back into our economy, thus boosting the health of our local economy.

Farmers' Market Salad (shop and make on the same day)

- 1 large cucumber, sliced in rounds, then cut in half
- 1-2 large fresh tomatoes, diced
- 1 small red onion, thinly sliced
- ½ cup goat cheese, broken in pieces
- 1-2 thick slices of fresh bread, cut into cubes
- High quality olive oil
- Fig balsamic vinegar

Toss all ingredients in a medium sized bowl, add salt and pepper to taste. Toss lightly with 2-3 tablespoons each of the olive oil and vinegar. Use salt and pepper as desired.

Health Hint

Many naturopaths say if women took selenium daily, we could wipe out 80% of breast cancer in just one generation. Selenium, a vital mineral, carries important antiviral properties and serves many purposes, including boosting cognitive function and immunity. It's effective against respiratory issues and, in high doses, helps fight cancer. Consider taking 200 mcg's daily.

Notes

◇◆◇

♡ Suns, Moons, and Success. Learn more: www.ChooseBigChange.com ♡

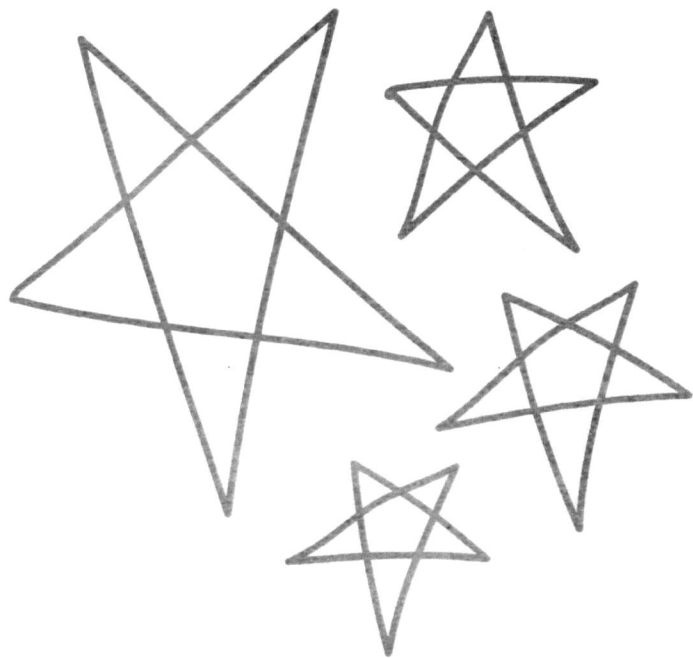

July

DISCORD, DISRUPTION, CHANGE

JULY 5–11

Do be willing to release old stories.
Do not be rigid in your thinking.

JULY 12–18

Do apply compassion and be creative in your goals.
Do not be apathetic.

JULY 19–25

Do seek middle ground.
Do not be insensitive to timing.

JULY 26–31, AUGUST 1

Do take time for relaxation.
Do not be too big for your britches.

THERE IS ONLY ONE RULE ON THIS *Wild Playground.* HAVE FUN, MY DEAR. *have fun!*

WHAT PATTERNS OF HARMONY CAN I BE AND RECEIVE?

JULY 9

NEW MOON 18° CANCER

Your Stable Future

JULY 23

FULL MOON 1° AQUARIUS

Seeking Flow

Energy Almanac 2021 EDITION

♡   Suns, Moons, and Success. Learn more: www.ChooseBigChange.com   ♡

July

◇◆◇

Solar Cycle:
3RD QUARTER
Keywords:
DISCORD, DISRUPTION, CHANGE

The beginning of July holds challenges, and the energies will feel similar to January. Look back at journals and notes you made at the time for a gentle reminder of what's ahead. Mars and Venus in Leo take turns reactivating the Saturn Uranus square, filling the first weeks of July with the passionate need to defend your own point of view. The situation is not helped by lack of clarity and possible deception during Mercury's square to Neptune.

In the midst of these potent planetary energies, the Cancer New Moon arrives on the 9th, and it's time to set intentions for security, home, family, and nurturing. An upturn comes mid-month when you may receive good news and some creative intuition. You may feel guided in the right direction. Ahh, optimism returns. Venus enters Virgo during week three, shifting our love nature and values to all things practical, organized, and perfecting while the Sun enters large-living Leo. Mercury shifts into dramatic Leo on the 27th. Jupiter retrogrades back into Aquarius and Mars is in opposition. Phew! There is potential for arguments around loyalty versus freedom. We'll breathe a sigh of relief when this roller coaster month ends.

DATES TO WATCH:

- **July 1-9 Mars square Saturn, Mars square Uranus, Sun sextile Uranus, Mercury square Neptune, Venus square Saturn, Venus square Uranus.** Nothing seems stable, and passionate desires face obstacles and shifts.
- **July 9 New Moon in Cancer.** *See July Moons section.*
- **July 13 Venus conjunct Mars.** Values and passions are in sync.
- **July 17 Sun in Cancer opposition Pluto.** Someone in a power position could reject your ideas about home and family.
- **July 22 Sun enters Leo.** Passion, creativity, and drama are highlighted.
- **July 23 Full Moon in Aquarius.** *See July Moons section.*
- **July 28 Jupiter retrogrades into Aquarius, Mars opposes Jupiter.** Expansion returns to technology, humanitarian ideas, and group-oriented topics but then faces immediate opposition.

JULY ASTROLOGY BY THE WEEKS

JULY 5-11

Lunar Signs:
TAURUS, GEMINI, CANCER, LEO
Lunar Cycle:
4TH QUARTER, NEW, 1ST QUARTER

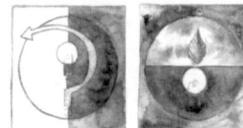

Sun sextile Uranus indicates helpful changes in home life. Mercury square Neptune creates confusing thoughts. Venus opposes Saturn, rejection of affection. Venus square Uranus warns of upsetting financial news. Mercury enters Cancer at week's end and thoughts become sentimental.

There's movement toward changes that can enhance security, and you may have some new ideas about finance and property. Put those new ideas to good use. But first, drop expectations, fact check information, and work on detachment before making any commitments or signing contracts. You may feel dampened in the areas of investment and relationship. This is followed by surprising change that can affect your relationships, finance, and values.

Moving into the New Moon, you may see something that needs to be released. You will naturally know what it is. Focus on setting intentions for home, family, and security. Mercury shifts into Cancer, and you may notice sentimental thoughts and conversations abound.

Shadow:
Inflexibility could be your downfall. Detach from a "my way is best" attitude and be willing to pivot.

JULY 12-18

Lunar Signs:
LEO, VIRGO, LIBRA, SCORPIO
Lunar Cycle:
1ST QUARTER, 2ND QUARTER

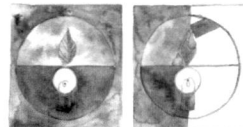

Mercury trine Jupiter brings optimism and good news. Venus conjunct Mars in Leo urges heightened creativity and romance. Sun trine Neptune brings visionary thoughts and ideals. Sun opposition Pluto, needs are blocked by authority.

Watch out! Flying high on feelings and visions, you may not be prepared for the conflict ahead.

The week begins with optimism, good news, and a beneficial combination of love and passion that supports the Leo areas of romance, entertainment, creative self-expression, parenting, and investment. This is a week where passionate love energy can create engagements and weddings or encourage the desire to start a family. Notice as your intuition guides your need for security at home. You can be swept away with positive visions and compassion. Enjoy this! Apply it to your personal growth and creative projects. But don't imagine these feelings are a guide to how everyone else is feeling now. Someone still in a power position has their focus on keeping that power. They surely won't be responsive to any appeals about sensitive topics.

Shadow:
Discouragement can lead to apathy. Trust that you always get what's best for you even if you can't see it right now. Alleviate resentment by any means possible. Try going for a run, journaling, or having a deep conversation with a trusted friend.

JULY 19-25	**Lunar Signs:** SCORPIO, SAGITTARIUS, CAPRICORN, AQUARIUS, PISCES **Lunar Cycle:** 2ND QUARTER, FULL, 3RD QUARTER

Mercury sextile Uranus, new ideas inspire change. Venus enters Virgo, creating a shift to practical values. Venus opposes Jupiter, love of order wrestles with expansion of the unknown. Sun enters Leo, intensifying self-expression. Full Moon in Aquarius polarizes self and group. Mercury trine Neptune seeks the ideal answer. Mercury opposition Pluto, a disappointing refusal.

The first few days of the third week in July brings along sensitivity, creativity, and psychic energy. Issues with family and your own feelings of security may be brought to light. Keep these feelings to yourself because someone prefers the status quo and doesn't approve. There is time to ponder all of this, and you can expect to receive inspiration about how to shift things for the better. When Venus enters Virgo at the end of the week, you can use these new ideas to improve your work and health. If you work at it, you may also boost your feelings of self-worth.

The Full Moon on the 23rd holds a dramatic Sun in Leo and a cool, detached Aquarius Moon. You may see fruition to some of your items on your Cancer New Moon list. Search for some middle ground now. Your personal desires and what's good for everyone are not the same thing. When sentimental dreams arrive, you may sense what is motivating others. This could fuel your own personal insecurities. If you communicate in an emotional way with someone in a position of power, you could end up disappointed. Practical non-emotional rapport is best.

Look at recent past experiences involving friends or group affiliations and consider how you might have a new point of view in these areas.

Shadow:
Manage your timing. Keep your eyes and ears open for clues that indicate a strategic time to approach an authority figure. It may be better to retreat and tweak the plan.

JULY 26-31, AUGUST 1	**Lunar Signs:** PISCES, ARIES, TAURUS **Lunar Cycle:** 3RD QUARTER, 4TH QUARTER

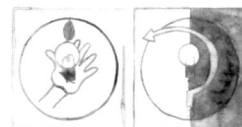

Mercury enters Leo for some dramatic thinking as Jupiter retrogrades into Aquarius, expanding group ideals. Venus squares the nodes, expressing with love can bring different ways of seeing. The Full Moon's polarity creates a change in the direction of action and passions. Sun and Mercury sextile North Node in Gemini, seeking new ideas for creative purposes. Sun conjunct Mercury, Mercury opposition Saturn, over identifying with thoughts may bring a pushback.

Overexertion and stress culminates midweek. Take time out to relax and cool down; let the future take care of itself for now. Your passion to lead is not appreciated when others want freedom of expression about their future plans. Temper your enthusiasm and allow in new ideas. If you let anger rule, you will miss the mark and regret the outcome. Be open to receiving information, including better ways to communicate. July ends in a more agreeable mode than it began. Spend your days recharging your spirit through activities with people on the same wavelength as you.

August begins with a warning to communicate carefully. Avoid any superior attitudes you have, or risk being met with rejection by others who are seeking a stronger group goal and identity.

Shadow:
Don't be too big for your britches! Relieve your need to be the leader and keep from going overboard by remembering that everyone has a point of view.

♡ Suns, Moons, and Success. Learn more: www.ChooseBigChange.com ♡

Energy Almanac 2021 Edition

Page 91

July Moons

NEW MOON IN 18° CANCER
JULY 9, 2021 9:16 PM EDT

Both the Sun and Moon approach an opposition to Pluto in Capricorn when the Cancer New Moon arrives. This transit creates discord between the needs of home, family, and security and the powers that be. You'll notice it in those intensely focused on public life and career. Do some goal setting that includes new ways to deal with finance, real estate, and values, but understand that there is a struggle with issues of investment and lessons concerning timing. Because there are no clear facts to work with, the best way now is to focus on the spiritual level. Spend time journaling and in meditation to receive inner guidance that will help you discover the right way forward.

FULL MOON IN 1° AQUARIUS
JULY 23, 2021 10:36 PM EDT

This Full Moon in Aquarius activates the differences between the need for independence, unique expression, and group affiliation (Aquarius) and creative self-expression, loyalty, romance, and children (Leo).

You can use your sensitive mind to receive spiritual input about how to ease any tensions that remain from earlier this month. Much of the stress energy has moved off.

Steer clear of overspending and don't allow others to take advantage of your desire to be helpful. You'll notice that a natural need to adjust is at play. It's time to get the everyday outer world, your spiritual nature, and your desire for leadership all working in harmony. Observe with detachment and make any adjustments.

23 Numerology

A 3 month in a 5 year. Use this vibrational energy to meditate using the affirmation "I Am a Creator". You are in control of everything in your life, and the dominant energy of 3 is amplifying your freedom of self-expression. You may feel yourself moved toward hands on creation or perhaps you'll rest into summer and use your mind to manifest something incredible. Adaptability will help you as you allow your intuition to guide you to activities that make you happy. Submit and trust that the universe is always working in your favor.

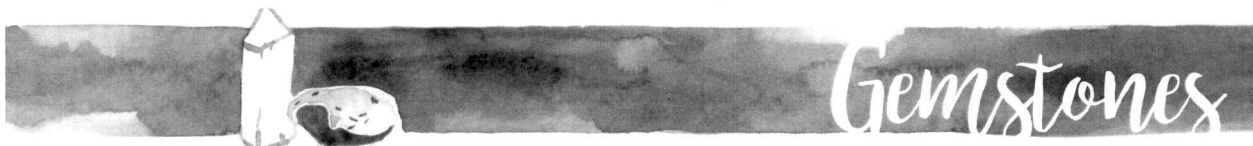

Gemstones

AQUAMARINE

Aquamarine is a stunning semi-translucent blue to blue-green stone with a refreshing energy that cools emotions and expands consciousness. Aquamarine activates both the throat and heart chakras, inspiring communication of your highest truth. Amid all of the stress, discord, and fluctuation, Aquamarine will soothe and nourish you. While it is a calming stone, it also maintains an alertness that aids in clarity and focus. This blend of energies is a wonderful combination during this month of disruption. Harnessing the water element, Aquamarine also connects you to the realms of the subconscious and the spirit. These realms are so powerful and can contribute greatly if you are willing to explore and shift. Aquamarine exudes cleansing energies. Use this stone daily for meditation and to release your emotions and limitations.

Keywords: SOOTHING, COMMUNICATION, AND CALMING.
Mantra: I EXPRESS THE DEPTHS OF MY BEING WITH CLARITY AND GRACE.

Essential Oils

This month you could find yourself taking an emotional roller coaster ride. The overall theme of the month is somewhat heavy, thereby inviting you to dig deep and feel all the feels. Not to fear, there are tools to support you through this turbulent time. Pairing oils with your favorite tried-and-true grounding practices will be of great benefit to you as you move through this month.

FOR TOPICAL USE

Sandalwood: Apply 1 drop on crown or forehead and over heart to induce a calm and quiet mind. Sandalwood helps align you with inner peace, tolerance, and love and aids you in slowing down and rebalancing the body. Use this powerful oil to aid you in all grounding practices.

DIFFUSE THIS BLEND

- Frankincense 2 drops
- Lime 2 drops
- Lavender 2 drops

Lower vibrations be gone! Frankincense, Lime, and Lavender mulled together and infused into the air will help release the heaviness you may be feeling this month. With the bright notes of Lime and the calming, comforting to the heart scent of Lavender you can ease yourself out of darkness and back into the light with the help of Frankincense which offers a multitude of benefits such as stress relief.

INGESTIBLE OPTIONS

Copaiba: Stress and nervous tension can dissipate with the use of the powerful oil Copaiba. Notice how it elevates your mood. Take 1 drop under the tongue or in a beverage.

Ginger: Ginger oil offers you strength and security. Take 1 drop under the tongue or add it to your favorite sparkling beverage. It's also delicious in a cup of hot tea with lemon.

♡ Suns, Moons, and Success. Learn more: www.ChooseBigChange.com ♡

Yoga

THE THREE DOSHAS OF AYURVEDA

doṣa: "fault, disease"

Learning about the three doshas of the Ayurveda system and, specifically, your personal dosha, can greatly compliment your yoga practice. Ayurveda is a type of alternative medicine that originated in India. Ayurveda literally means knowledge of life. A dosha is a metabolic type according to your physical and mental makeup. There are three doshas in this system. Although all three doshas are present in all of us, we are typically dominant in one or two main doshas. By knowing your dominant dosha(s), you may learn how to best balance your health.

Each of the doshas thrive with a specific diet, lifestyle, and exercise regimen for best health. If an imbalance is presented in your life, you can use the knowledge of your dosha(s) to help correct it.

THE CHARACTERISTICS OF EACH DOSHA

Use the following list to help determine which dosha or combination of doshas you might be.

- **Vata Dosha:** Vata types tend toward slenderness with prominent features. They can be moody, energetic, and impulsive. They are often very enthusiastic about new projects. Vata types need quiet when eating so as not to get too distracted and thus disturbing their digestion. Foods that balance Vata are warm, grounding, sweet, and contain healthy fats. One-pot dishes suit Vata types well. Minimize foods that are cold, dry, and raw.

    Best Yoga Asanas to Balance Vata: The best asanas to balance a Vata type are grounding poses. Some examples: Uttanasana (Standing Forward Bend), Balasana (Child's Pose), and Padmasana (Lotus Pose).

- **Pitta Dosha:** Pitta types typically have a medium build and are well proportioned. They tend to keep a stable weight through their adult lives. They are deep sleepers and are prone to vivid dreams. Flavors associated with balancing Pitta are cooling, sweet, bitter, and astringent. Pittas tend toward eating raw foods. Pittas need to stay away from stimulating foods such as alcohol and coffee.

    Best Yoga Asanas to Balance Pitta: Asanas that have a calming effect will best suit the restless pitta mind. Some examples: Ustrasana (Camel Pose), Duanurasna (Bow Pose), and Bhujangasana (Cobra Pose).

- **Kapha Dosha:** Kapha types tend to be heavier and solidly built. Although strong, kaphas tend toward overeating. Kaphas are balanced by spicy, bitter, or astringent foods. Fresh ginger is especially beneficial for balancing kapha types. Reduce foods that are heavy such as red meat and fried, fatty foods.

    Best Yoga Asanas to Balance Kapha: Kapha types will benefit greatly from stimulating and heating asanas. Some examples are Setu Bandha (Bridge Pose) and the entire Sun Salutation sequence.

Chew on This

Greek Physician Hippocrates said, "Let food be thy medicine and medicine be thy food". We often forget to boost our immunity in the middle of summer, but how many of you have caught that summer cold? It's the worst! As you pack your cooler for the beach, barbeque, or camping, be sure to bring these immunity boosting foods for you and the kids.

Snacks: Oranges, bananas, apples, pineapple, blueberries, grapes, pumpkin seeds.

Salads: Use dark leafy greens (spinach and kale), onions, and bell peppers. Choose red, yellow and orange; they make your salad bright and colorful!

For the grill: Eggplant, portobello mushrooms, chicken, and beef.

Other delicious immunity boosters: Oysters, mussels, and clams.

Immunity Boosting Smoothie
Using some of the ingredients above, enjoy this huge dose of anti-inflammatory, cancer-fighting flavonoids and 100% of your recommended daily dose of superstar antioxidant vitamin C. *Makes 2 Servings (20 to 24 ounces).*

- 1 large banana (fresh or frozen)
- ¾ cup frozen mango cubes (or use pineapple)
- 2 cups spinach, tightly packed
- 1 teaspoon hemp seeds (optional, but highly recommended)
- 1 ⅔ cups nondairy milk of choice
- Blend, serve, and boost!

Health Hint

The human body begins losing its natural capacity to retain vitamins by our second decade. A multivitamin gives your body a little bit of everything it needs to be high functioning and is beneficial for life in our high-stress society. Seek a high quality, organic brand and take the recommended dosage.

♡ Suns, Moons, and Success. Learn more: www.ChooseBigChange.com ♡

Energy Almanac 2021 EDITION

Page 95

Notes

—◇◆◇—

_____
_____
_____
_____
_____
_____
_____
_____
_____
_____
_____
_____
_____
_____
_____
_____
_____
_____
_____
_____
_____
_____
_____
_____
_____
_____
_____

Grab your free bonuses here: www.ChooseBigChange.com/bonus21

August

REAPING, ORGANIZING, PRESERVING

AUGUST 2-8

Do follow intuitive inspirations.
Do not be overly dramatic.

AUGUST 9-15

Do detach from irritations.
Do not be overly critical of others.

AUGUST 16-22

Do seek compromise.
Do not avoid self-analysis.

AUGUST 23-29

Do lay the groundwork for beneficial relationships.
Do not become complacent.

AUGUST 30-31, SEPTEMBER 1-5

Do gather more information before taking action.
Do not avoid your authentic feelings about recent events.

gratitude IS WINE FOR THE SOUL. GO ON. GET DRUNK.

HOW CAN ORDER CONTRIBUTE TO MY LIFE?

AUGUST 8

NEW MOON IN 16° LEO

Peaceful Solutions

AUGUST 22

FULL MOON IN 29° AQUARIUS

Freedom & Self-Expression

♡ Suns, Moons, and Success. Learn more: www.ChooseBigChange.com ♡

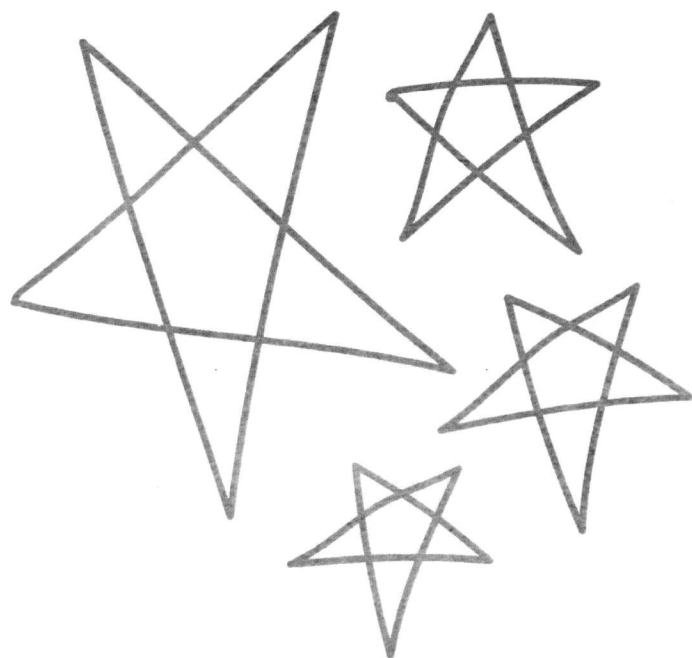

August

———— ◇◇◇ ————

Solar Cycle:
3RD QUARTER
Keywords:
REAPING ORGANIZING PRESERVING

The month of August, though not as intense as July, gives little time to readjust from last month's challenges. In the waning solar cycle, all outer planets will be in retrograde. Uranus retrograde, agent of change, is at play. It rules electronic devices, so it is wise to prepare for any possible technology issues and purchase televisions, computers, and all electronics before backward motion begins. Uranus will remain retrograde in Taurus for the rest of the year.

Harvest time begins with Venus and Mars in Virgo. This brings energy that assists with organizing, perfecting, and preserving supplies and sources of sustenance. Mercury (on the 11th) and the Sun (on the 22nd) also enter Virgo, sign of work and health. During the Virgo influence, you can evaluate your progress, notice how you might perfect your endeavors, and look at any preparations or maintenance needed for the rest of the year. It's also a good time to check in on your health and find ways to improve well-being. The downside comes when each Virgo planet opposes Neptune, resulting in confusion and illusion.

Venus enters Libra on the 16th after which love and values focus on relationship, agreements, contracts, legal issues, harmony, and beauty. Charm will bring you helpful outcomes during negotiations. A desire to relax in the sun accompanies August's Leo New Moon on the 8th. The Full Moon in the last degree of Aquarius on the 22nd is the second Full Moon in this sign. While they get no fanfare, a second Full Moon in any sign carries more significance than a second Full Moon in a calendar month (known as the Blue Moon). The sign's double emphasis means having a second chance to experience the meaning of the polarity. Could there be an improvement of the harvest?

DATES TO WATCH:

- **August 1-2 Mercury opposes Saturn, Sun opposes Saturn.** A desire for affection and entertainment is blocked by duties to groups. It's not the time for proposals.

- **August 6-7 Sun squares Uranus.** The expression of affection and desire for loyalty clashes with independent values.

- **August 8 Leo New Moon.** *See August Moons section.*

- **Aug 9-11 Venus opposition Neptune, Mercury opposition Jupiter.** Over-idealization and too much optimism may cloud decision making.

- **August 18-20 Mercury conjunct Mars, Sun opposes Jupiter.** If you push too hard for affection or personal desires, you may experience a pullback.

- **August 22 Aquarius Full Moon.** *See August Moons section.*

- **August 24-25 Mercury opposition Neptune.** Facts are distorted and communication with others is unreliable. Local travel hits snags.

♡ Suns, Moons, and Success. Learn more: www.ChooseBigChange.com ♡

Energy Almanac 2021 EDITION

Page 99

AUGUST ASTROLOGY BY THE WEEKS

AUGUST 2-8, 2021

Lunar Signs:
TAURUS, GEMINI, CANCER, LEO
Lunar Cycle:
4TH QUARTER, NEW

Sun opposes Saturn concerns self versus group. Venus trine Uranus, changes improve security. Mercury square Uranus, change upsets ideas. Sun square Uranus brings a clash of wills. New Moon in Leo.

If you want specific future results, avoid drama and self-interest. This isn't a week to seek commitment or affection in relationships.

If so inspired, make changes in the realm of finance, home, garden, diet, and values. It's a good use of your time. Expect surprising changes to conflict with your personal desires again as the week goes on. In this, the last quarter phase, you become aware of things that need to change or be released. Form your intentions for passion, creativity, and entertainment at the Leo New Moon.

Shadow:
Overdramatizing doesn't help. Self-check regularly to see if you are embellishing just to get your way. Report your stories from a place of calm.

AUGUST 9-15

Lunar Signs:
LEO, VIRGO, LIBRA, SCORPIO, SAGITTARIUS
Lunar Cycle:
1ST QUARTER, 2ND QUARTER

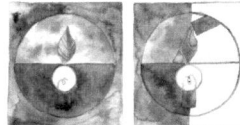

Venus opposite Neptune and Mars square the nodes creates idealization and frustration in communications. Mercury opposite Jupiter, Mercury enters Virgo, you may feel overly optimistic until thinking shifts to a practical mode. Venus trine Pluto, a powerful person returns. Mercury square Nodes and soon logic is needed to sort things out.

Don't try to make sense of things or find direction until help arrives on Wednesday. Try to detach from irritation which may arise over disorganization and feeling let down when things aren't working perfectly as this week begins. Overcompensation for stress can appear as optimism about the future. Be realistic about the situation. Fortunately, your thinking will quickly come back down to earth and you can focus on mundane matters in an organized way.

You'll find it helpful if you revisit ideas of renovation, reorganization, and renewal in the areas of work, health, and career. Pay attention! Is there a romantic bond forming that also supports your goals in work and health? By Sunday you find it hard to deal with things when others have widely different viewpoints, but don't criticize because that never helps. Carefully analyze before you choose between opposite perspectives.

Shadow:
Believing the unbelievable can lead to let down. Release attachment to unrealistic methods and people. Apply practical thinking whenever you can.

✵ www.TheEnergyAlmanac.com ✵

AUGUST 16-22

Lunar Signs:
SAGITTARIUS, CAPRICORN, AQUARIUS, PISCES
Lunar Cycle:
2ND QUARTER

Venus enters Libra and charm soothes over critical observations. Mercury conjunct Mars delivers sharp, judgmental words. Sun opposition Jupiter, Mercury trine Uranus has you looking for the best possible solutions. Venus trine North Node finds points of agreement. Mars trine Uranus, Full Moon in Aquarius, Sun enters Virgo, all on the 22nd, creating a passion to bring order out of chaos but meets with intense feelings of polarity between self and group.

It might take a while for it to activate, but use this week to seek kinder ways to relate and to focus on compromise.

Your best ideas are lacking clarity and support on Wednesday. The Virgo perfectionist attitude may find you feeling frustrated. Don't be surprised if critical communications go out of bounds again on Thursday. Take a solo approach to work. Address projects that require analysis and/or hand-eye coordination. This will keep you busy until the emotional storm cloud passes. When a silver lining appears, find ways to implement changes in finance, health, home, and work.

If you use sweet words on Saturday, you may incite compromise and better relations. Notice as your feelings intensify around the Aquarius Full Moon and you feel ready to work things out in a practical way. Thankfully, discord always cools under self-analysis.

Shadow:
Perfectionism is problematic. Being overly critical of self or others creates undue stress. Do some deep breathing or use EFT (Emotional Freedom Technique) to distract yourself in the moment and remember to let everyone perform at their own pace.

AUGUST 23-29

Lunar Signs:
PISCES, ARIES, TAURUS, GEMINI
Lunar Cycle:
3RD QUARTER

Venus trine Saturn, kind words heal relationship difficulties. Mercury opposes Neptune, you can't follow directions when they aren't clear. Mercury trine Pluto finds a way to put things back in place. Sun squares the nodes, logic could be applied to end conflicts over beliefs and facts.

Start the week ready to make agreements and lay the groundwork for relationships that will further your future goals. If you receive misinformation, you might experience a brief setback on Wednesday. Take the time on Thursday to review situations with someone you trust. A few quiet days will allow you time for implementation and assimilation of strategies.

Hold tight as the week closes. Sunday brings another conflict to light. This time the discussion is about perceptions and beliefs versus detailed fact-finding. Lean into the situation by applying organized analysis which may reveal a way to include both.

Shadow:
Complacency is the enemy of success. Agreeing for harmony's sake won't serve the greater good. Maintain healthy boundaries and gently speak your mind as needed.

♡ Suns, Moons, and Success. Learn more: www.ChooseBigChange.com ♡

Energy Almanac 2021 Edition

Page 101

AUGUST 30-31, SEPTEMBER 1-5

Lunar Signs:
TAURUS, GEMINI
Lunar Cycle:
3RD QUARTER, 4TH QUARTER

Mercury enters Libra, you find yourself weighing pros and cons. Thursdays' Mars opposition Neptune is not a time for action; wait for more information. Mercury trine Saturn brings clarity and the way to proceed. The last days of August contain no planetary aspects, but still echo the irritation encountered when thoughts and beliefs are not in sync.

Focus now on exploring how you authentically feel about the harvest of this year. List what you'd like to change for next year before you move on to September. Use creative energy for organization and preparation for the months ahead. Seek ways to balance your thoughts and enhance harmony in all areas. It's a good time for a relaxing, long weekend vacation. When Thursday arrives, remember that if the way ahead is not clear, don't make a move. Let the moment pass, then get more information and have another look at goals and priorities regarding group affiliations. Be prepared and reap great results by creating an organized plan.

The tone is set for September. Rest and enjoy the quiet days. This will allow for adjustment to a new way of thinking and communicating. You will be expected to act on Thursday, but there could be some confusion about what is expected. Seek more information and the situation will be resolved.

Shadow:
Overanalyzing and second guessing the past may stall your progress. Use mindfulness practices to stay in the present time.

August Moons

NEW MOON IN 16° LEO
AUGUST 8, 2021 1:49 PM EDT

When the Leo New Moon arrives, you should set intentions for creative self-expression, romance, children, entertainment, and investment (all areas that Leo rules). If you look ahead and see that personal desires conflict with changes happening in finance and values, it could be uncomfortable.

Be mindful of being overly optimistic. What you desire may not be what the group wants.

Uranus in Taurus is still in orb of the square to Saturn in Aquarius. This transit is an opportunity to resolve changes by applying a steady, wise approach to the future. Mars and Venus in perfection-seeking Virgo put emphasis on analyzing and organization. This combination brings friction between different ways of seeing the world.

Don't let your good judgment be overpowered by idealization and false representations. Set an intention to find peaceful, balanced solutions in relationships of all kinds. It may bear fruit at the Full Moon later this month.

_____
_____
_____
_____

Grab your free bonuses here: www.ChooseBigChange.com/bonus21

FULL MOON IN 29° AQUARIUS
AUGUST 22, 2021 12:01 AM EDT

This second Full Moon in Aquarius gives us a second attempt at resolving the polarity between the need for forward-thinking ideals, freedom, unique expression, and group affiliations, versus identity with self-expression, personal creativity, loyalty, and parenting. This fixed tug of war is enhanced with the Sun on fixed star Regulus. Regulus means "Little Prince." It enhances the special focus of Leo. The Aquarius lunar energy is amplified by the Moon conjunct Jupiter, ruler of the gods. It feels like there is royalty in the room.

There could be a major standoff now among "monarchs" (think leaders or authorities) who are unwilling to give up their position or reach any compromise. In home life, think parents and the oldest child. In the outer world, think bosses or government officials.

Thankfully, other not-so-royal planets have moved on to help you find workable solutions. Stay alert because information could be cloudy due to Neptune's position. Expect help from Venus energy. She just wants to assist in negotiating peace for a stable future.

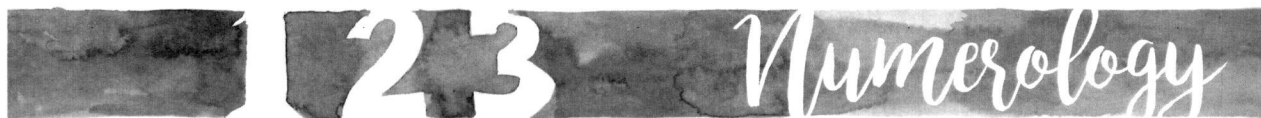

_____

_____

_____

_____

23 Numerology

A 4 month in a 5 year. This month's four energy helps solidify foundations in your life. It is time to consider embracing alternative options to create your future. Write down your design to manifest what you want in your life in a practical manner. The four energy calls for logic. Make plans while keeping in mind that everything is a process. Getting down to the details is essential in manifesting your goals in physical form.

Suns, Moons, and Success. Learn more: www.ChooseBigChange.com

Energy Almanac 2021 Edition

Page 103

Gemstones

JADE

Jade is a gorgeous green stone. By simply looking at Jade, you can perceive its power as it is the ultimate stone of well-being. Jade activates the heart chakra and is known for its healing capacities in this area. With Mercury in Virgo, Jade offers us the possibility to nurture our health and well-being. It will also contribute flow and ease as you journey through obstacles and illusions. This stone is great for meditation and may be worn during sleep and out in nature. Harnessing the earth element, Jade draws in the earth's energy and enhances the growth of your life force.

Keywords: HEALTH AND ABUNDANCE
Mantra: I FLOW ENERGY FROM THE EARTH, HEALING ALL MY IMBALANCES.

Essential Oils

In the heat of this month, we are being met with a much gentler energy, and we are being given the opportunity to slow down and rebound from last month's challenges. You are being prompted to focus on health and well-being and ways to better support yourself in this area.

FOR TOPICAL USE

Eucalyptus: Apply over lungs and chest.** Eucalyptus encourages us to take full responsibility for our health and aids in opening up and clearing the brain. For those with sensitive skin, you may wish to dilute eucalyptus with a carrier oil such as fractionated coconut oil or oil of your choice. Always use a carrier oil when using oils with children. **Refer to the safety with oils article in the front of this almanac.

Melaleuca: Apply 1-3 drops to the bottom of feet or crown of head. Tea Tree Oil, this oil's common name, is for creating healthy boundaries and assists you in purification and release.

DIFFUSE THIS BLEND

- **Lemon 2 drops**
- **Grapefruit 2 drops**
- **Cypress 1 drop**

Support your mind, body, and spirit with this citrusy blend. Lemon restores energy and bestows clarity as Grapefruit helps in honoring the body. Cypress works with the heart and mind by moving energy throughout your body, creating openness.

INGESTIBLE OPTIONS

Grapefruit: This citrus oil is used to support bringing focus to your health and wellness. Take 1-2 drops under the tongue or in a beverage.

THE KING OF HIP OPENERS: PIGEON POSE

Eka Pāda Rājakapotāsana, eka: "one"; *pada:* "foot"; *raja:* "king"; *kapota:* "pigeon"; *asana:* "pose"

Through the summer months, one can tend toward overdoing it physically. In turn, your joints, muscles, and tendons start to feel the stress of the heightened activity. And quite often, it's our hips that take the brunt of the stress of our bodies. By balancing and easing hip pain, we can often alleviate joint pain in the legs, ease lower back pain, and relax psoas muscles and hip flexors. By performing Pigeon Pose we can ease these muscle and joint problems. It's no wonder that Pigeon is often a yogi's favorite pose for all the benefits that it provides.

Please take in this pose carefully if you suffer from any knee pain. If you start to feel any intense pain in your knees, ease out of the pose gently and try performing the pose in a reclined position on your back. (This alternative pose is called "thread the needle".)

PIGEON POSE

1. Come to all fours on the ground. Bring your right knee in toward your right wrist placing it on the ground in front of it. The side of your right leg will be on the floor. Don't worry if you cannot come all the way toward your wrist; come as far as you can. Your right ankle will be somewhere close to your left hip (advanced students can bring their foot closer to their left wrist.)

2. Slide your right leg back and point your toes with the sole of your foot facing toward the ceiling.

3. Feel your hips coming square with one another. Ease them down and forward. You may use some support under your buttock if needed (such as a rolled-up towel).

4. Inhale and lift your hands slightly so that only your fingertips are on the ground and push up gently, feeling your body respond to the movement pushing the torso out.

5. As you exhale, place or walk your hands forward and lower your upper body toward the floor as best you can. Rest your forearms and forehead on the ground.

6. Stay here and breathe for about six or seven breaths or as long as you wish. Pay attention to any tension in your hips and gently ease them by consciously releasing the muscles around them.

7. To come out of the pose, push into your hands, lift your upper body away from the ground slightly until your hips raise up, and move back onto all fours. Repeat on the other side.

♡ Suns, Moons, and Success. Learn more: www.ChooseBigChange.com ♡

Page 105

Chew on This

Contrary to popular belief, nutrition is a secondary source of energy. Primary foods, or non-food sources of nourishment, are what really fuel us. As children, we all lived on primary food when we would play outside for countless hours, enjoying hobbies and creative activity. Think about your relationships. How "ful-filled" are you while being in love? Consider your career or business and the passion that fuels the work you do. The buzz and excitement of daily life can feed us more completely than any food.

As we work through the layers of life, nourishment and self-care, evaluate these four areas of "soul food":

- **Career.** Do you love the work you do? Are you doing the work you love? You can have both.

- **Spirituality.** This can mean anything you want it to; it doesn't have to be religious. Spirituality is the celebration of being connected to one another and everything around us. The practice of spirituality can be grounding and help provide a sense of meaning and belonging. It's exactly what we need right now.

- **Relationships.** Partner, parents, children, self. Do one or several of these need some work or a good talk?

- **Physical activity.** How are you moving your body? Which way does your body crave to move?

The more primary food we give ourselves, the less we depend on food to make us feel good. As well, the more we reach for food to "fill up", we leave less room and awareness for primary food, our true source of nourishment. Many religions and cultures practice fasting to reduce overeating, thus opening channels to receive a greater amount of "soul food". Take some quality time to explore your personal balance between primary food and actual food. Which area could use some attention?

Health Hint

Did you know your body needs iodine but actually can't make it? Research shows that 90% of the world population is low on iodine. The glut of thyroid issues among people is good proof. This chemical element must come via food or supplementation. Iodine helps fuel the thyroid which acts as a regulator in your body. With low thyroid function you'll notice cold extremities and lethargy among other issues. Kale, shrimp, cod, eggs, prunes, and kelp will help increase our iodine levels, but liquid iodine as a supplement is an easier way to go. Follow the recommended dosage on the product you purchase.

Notes

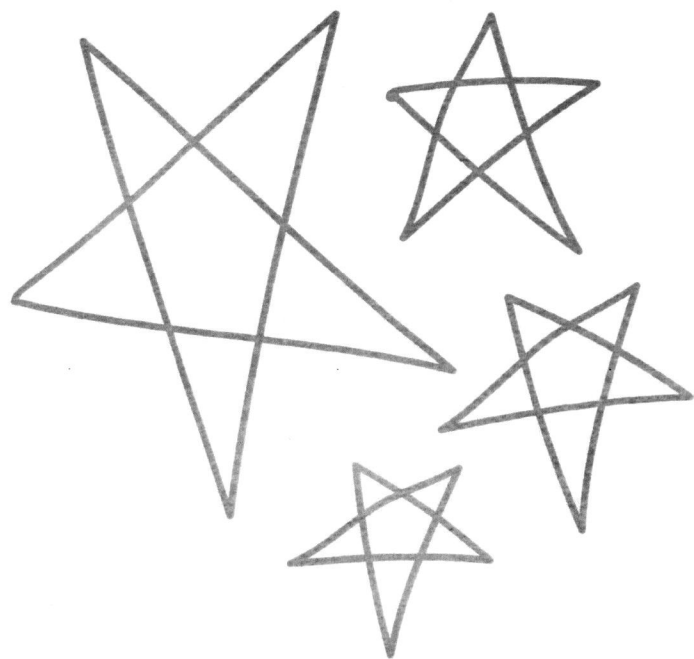

September

RELATIONSHIP, ADJUSTMENT, AUTHENTICITY

SEPTEMBER 6-12

Do seek tools and resources.
Do not be secretive or manipulative.

SEPTEMBER 13-19

Do wait for any confusion to clear.
Do not get stuck overanalyzing.

SEPTEMBER 20-26

Do apply logical analysis to situations.
Do not avoid your psychic capacities.

SEPTEMBER 27-30, OCTOBER 1-3

Do review and reflect.
Do not overdo.

Bend,
or
you'll
break.

WHAT CAN I BE OR DO DIFFERENTLY THAT WILL CREATE IN A WHOLE NEW WAY?

SEPTEMBER 6

NEW MOON IN 14° VIRGO
New Ways to Work

SEPTEMBER 20

FULL MOON IN 28° PISCES
Applied Logical & Intuitive Skills

Energy Almanac 2021 EDITION

♡   Suns, Moons, and Success. Learn more: www.ChooseBigChange.com   ♡

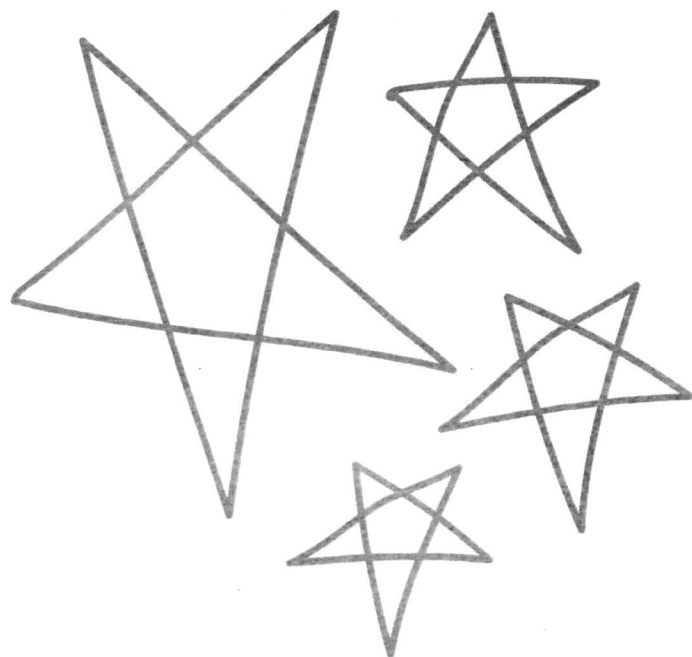

September

Solar Cycle: 3RD QUARTER **Equinox:** 4TH QUARTER
Keywords:
REAPING ORGANIZING PRESERVING

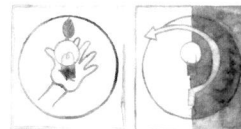

The sun's rays are still in Virgo as September begins, supporting your focus on school and work and the necessary preparations for a new season ahead. In the northern hemisphere, the solar cycle is getting close to a shift from the lighter half to darker half of the solar year.

The Autumnal Equinox occurs at the point of equal light and dark hours when the Sun enters Libra on the 22nd at 3:21 p.m. Eastern. The darkest half begins, and all outer planets retrograde. You'll feel a natural pull to turn inward. This supports looking back over the year to see if what you've achieved actually reflects your original goals. You may also explore whether these goals are still true to your authentic self after all the experiences and growth of 2021. While you ponder, you may discover where an adjustment is needed for 2022.

In the same way, you'll be inclined to look at relationship issues to see where adjustments can be made to create greater harmony or whether it's time for a peaceful parting of the ways. After Mars enters Libra on the 14th, areas of discord become more apparent. The idea of balance underlies many thoughts and experiences. Review is further supported when Mercury slows down for retrograde motion on the 27th.

Venus enters Scorpio on the 10th, and your love nature shifts to deep emotional waters. Commitment is part of Scorpio energy as is the use of shared resources. With Venus here, you'll explore how to engage lovingly with the values of others. This transit is until October 7th which gives you plenty of time to detect where manipulation, obsession, and control are underlying factors in your life. You could now see how to evolve and regenerate experiences.

It's good to know that despite some bumps along the way, September ends in a peaceful and uplifting energy.

DATES TO WATCH:

- **September 1-3 Mars opposition Neptune.** A desire for precision is frustrated by confusion.

- **September 5 Venus squares Pluto.** Relationships conflict with public life.

- **September 6 Virgo New Moon.** *See September Moons section.*

- **September 10 Venus enters Scorpio.** Values and love nature shift.

- **September 13-14 Sun opposition Neptune, Mars enters Libra.** Confusion makes organization difficult. Passions shift.

- **September 16-17 Venus square Saturn.** Manipulation tactics are blocked by fixed ideas and plans for the future.

- **September 20 Pisces Full Moon.** *See September Moons section.*

- **September 21-30 Mercury square Pluto, Venus opposes Uranus. Mercury slows down and retrogrades.** Thoughts and communications about justice, relationship, and cooperation are blocked by an authority. There's also a surprising shift in relationship and/or finance.

- **September 22 Autumnal Equinox.** Day and night are equal length, and so begins the waning of light.

- **September 27 Mercury retrogrades in Libra.** Review relationships and legal matters.

♡ Suns, Moons, and Success. Learn more: www.ChooseBigChange.com ♡

SEPTEMBER ASTROLOGY BY THE WEEKS

SEPTEMBER 6-12

Lunar Signs:
VIRGO, LIBRA, SCORPIO, SAGITTARIUS
Lunar Cycle:
4TH QUARTER, NEW, 1ST QUARTER

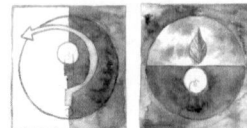

Pluto is at play this week. Pushing too hard can counteract steady progress. A wish is granted but dreams may be too big. New Moon and Sun trine Uranus; there's a chance to plan and begin a new cycle. Venus enters Scorpio, intensifying expressions of love and commitment.

If you see that steady progress is being achieved in practical ways, don't push for your own need for security. You may find something you'd hoped for comes back into the picture.

The Virgo New Moon begs you to set intentions to restore organization and good health habits. Allow new values to be part of your new regime regarding finance, home, possessions, work, and health. You can move forward with your intentions without obstacles and seek resources needed during the peaceful days that follow.

Venus enters Scorpio on Friday, and you will find strong feelings about shared finances, intimacy, and commitment start to show up. The deep emotions of this secretive Venus energy can cause problems if you're not aware of the potentials for manipulation and obsession that can underlie behaviors. If you explore this energy carefully, you may find that motivations are based on vulnerability. Understanding this will benefit all involved.

Shadow:
Manipulation is harmful. Stay wise to underlying motivations, yours and that of others. Your opportunity for truthful negotiations is at hand.

SEPTEMBER 13-19

Lunar Signs:
SAGITTARIUS, CAPRICORN, AQUARIUS, PISCES
Lunar Cycle:
2ND QUARTER

Sun opposes Neptune and creates difficulty in organizing. Mars enters Libra, bringing passion into relationships and discussions. Sun trine Pluto, Venus square Saturn, has you making headway with goals, but issues of control could arise.

As the week begins, organization and logic are illusive, and it's best to wait for this cloud to pass before moving forward. Once Mars shifts into Libra, you'll see how arguing for a cause can bring more resistance than agreement. In discussions of contracts and partnership, you might get to take action but not before handling some arguments. Breathe deep; this too shall pass.

You sure are passionate these days, but remember to apply logical analysis. It will help you make headway, and you can begin renovations to improve forms, systems, or structures for outer life goals.

You may be wondering how to secure future plans, particularly around shared resources. There could be a snag in the deal. Someone isn't "all in". Process all of this before the next week begins.

Shadow:
Be wary of too much analyzing and too little spiritual focus. Balance the focus on mundane concerns with meditation and request for guidance.

SEPTEMBER 20-26

Lunar Signs:
PISCES, ARIES, TAURUS, GEMINI
Lunar Cycle:
FULL, 3RD QUARTER

Mercury trine Jupiter is good news. The Pisces Full Moon invokes intense feelings. Mars trine North Node helps with receiving good ideas, then communications are negative when Mercury squares Pluto. Sun enters Libra at the Autumnal Equinox. Venus opposition Uranus causes surprising shifts. Mars trine Saturn finds ways to work things out.

Be mindful of your approach when communicating this week. Good ideas are helpful, but there is some tension between what is logical and what are psychic feelings. As you enter the last solar quarter at the Equinox, look at challenges to commitments and disagreements about finance. Apply logical analysis in order to reach the best deal.

Engage in positive communications on the 20th, especially with friends and groups. It's a good day to see people eye to eye about future goals. The Full Moon reveals where you'll need to find a compromise between logical analysis and acting through inner guidance. Seek harmony through information that could lead to contracts and agreements but know that you could face one powerful pundit that may not hear your point of view. Serious discrepancies about values, finance, and/or partnership commitments cause disruption in any or all of these areas. Your desire to reach peace is empowered when you take positive steps to review and weigh timing and practices for future goals. Trust that you can be successful in finding positive ways to express this and eventually reach agreements.

Shadow:
Do not fear tapping into your psychic side. Your spiritual self is available to help your more logical side if you'll take the time to tune in.

SEPTEMBER 27-30, OCTOBER 1-3

Lunar Signs:
GEMINI, CANCER, LEO, VIRGO
Lunar Cycle:
4TH QUARTER

Sun trine North Node and Mercury retrogrades, more helpful details are received as the mind internalizes to review the past weeks. Venus trine Neptune, Sun trine Saturn, creative ideas and good meetings are had. Venus square Jupiter causes overdoing. Mercury square Pluto, Venus sextile Pluto invokes difficulty with discussions.

The last days of September hold more review and re-do energy. There are positive visions and the understanding of how to implement them, but you should still hold off on being overly optimistic. October begins with lessons in the art of communication.

In the waning lunar cycle, you are looking at authenticity and which things need to be released or cleared. This sudden shift reveals where those needs lie. Typically, in the last quarter of the solar cycle, you begin to look ahead for the next year to come. New information will help formulate the details, but Mercury stops and retrogrades. This transit causes a need for you to rethink ideas and decisions formed this month. Mercury retrograde can bring up old arguments internally, or externally, and it's possible an old relationship returns to your life.

Channel your dreams and fantasies about love into creative projects where you may discover new ways to present and produce your visions. This gives you time to receive guidance when reviewing future plans regarding all things Libra (relationship, partnerships, and/or contracts and legal issues.) Psychic and spiritual energy can be used to provide insights for healing emotions and issues regarding personal values. Everyone is having intense emotions now, and someone may feel their independent ideas of the future are threatened. For a green light, present different ideas and points of view carefully. Use gentle persuasion about how you can incorporate shared values and use shared resources for financial success.

Shadow:
Feeling out of control can set off overdoing. Don't force things. Meditate for guidance on timing and becoming peaceful with current differences.

♡ Suns, Moons, and Success. Learn more: www.ChooseBigChange.com ♡

September Moons

NEW MOON IN 14° VIRGO
SEPTEMBER 6, 2021 8:51 PM EDT

When the Virgo New Moon arrives, set intentions for work, health, mentorship, and being complete within yourself. The Sun and Moon trine Uranus in Taurus open you up to new ways to organize at home and work. It may also help you deal with health.

Mercury trine Saturn brings positive thoughts and communications about ways to implement future goals regarding relationship, contracts, and legal matters. You will feel a positive uplift in those areas but do be careful of setting your expectations too high. You have the skills and support to make any needed changes which surely will help.

Venus is squaring Pluto and Mars is opposite Neptune so there may be stumbling blocks and confusion that you must muddle through. Apply your best Virgo traits to work through it.

FULL MOON IN 28° PISCES
SEPTEMBER 20, 2021 7:54 PM EDT

Remember, all Full Moons represent an opposition between the Sun and Moon. The Full Moon in Pisces brings the need to reconcile the differences between spirituality, retreat, and inner life (Pisces) versus identity with work, health, analyzing, perfecting and organizing (Sun in Virgo). The Moon is also joined with Neptune which enhances the dreamy inner world quality.

You may feel fueled to apply orderly perfection to relationships and agreements. This is because the Sun in Virgo is in out-of-sign conjunction to Mars. Fortunately, Sun and Moon positively aspect Pluto in Capricorn. Some reconciliation comes when you review needed change (Pluto) in structures, logic, and timing (Capricorn).

An issue may arise from the fixed T-square formed by Venus' opposition to Uranus, both square Saturn. If you'll come to the table with willingness and wanting to work at it, you can come to an agreement. Topics include commitments, finance, values, and the future. Mercury's trine to Jupiter suggests counseling or a mediator can take some of the pressure off. Try to remember things you agreed upon in the past.

✵ www.TheEnergyAlmanac.com ✵

723 Numerology

A 5 month in a 5 year. Expect a diversity of experiences to occur which will urge you toward change. This electric energy can be used in creating products of the mind such as an invention, a book or creative composition, or, more likely, plans for an adventure. Use concentration to focus or you risk getting nothing done this month. Your desire to move and shake may require a little taming or the need for flexibility.

Gemstones

BRONZITE

Bronzite is a brown stone with golden flecks. It is often overlooked. However, this stone has been used for thousands of years and holds great grounding energy for activating the root chakra and second chakra. These energetic aspects will contribute greatly to the month of September. Bronzite will encourage clarity and flow, especially through the distraction of perfectionism. It also restores harmony amid discord within oneself and with those around you. Be sure to carry this stone with you for more ease. Harnessing the earth element, Bronzite enhances loving discernment which aids in working with others.

Keywords: CLARITY, COURTESY, AND CERTAINTY
Mantra: MY ACTIONS ARE CLEAR AND REFLECT THE FLOW OF THE UNIVERSE.

Essential Oils

As the days get shorter and nights get longer, we move into the darkest part of the year. As with nature, we are invited to go in, slow down, and reflect. In this space, you can discover where adjustments need to be made and whether or you are living as your authentic self. To do so will require the quieting of an overactive mind, the release of the need for perfection, and finding balance and harmony within yourself.

FOR TOPICAL USE

Magnolia: Apply 1-2 drops over the heart or to the crown of the head. This oil supports the heart/mind connection and inspires you to see the beauty within each individual.

Ravensara: *Do not use if pregnant or nursing.* Apply 1-2 drops around the navel or to bottoms of feet. Using this oil helps in quieting the mind and calls forth inner peace.

DIFFUSE THIS BLEND

- **Coriander 3 drops**
- **Vetiver 2 drops**
- **Geranium 1 drop**

Support yourself during September's darkening days with a grounding blend whose aroma helps foster trust, living authentically, and relieving stress and tension. This beautiful blend is supportive for your personal journey.

INGESTIBLE OPTIONS

Cassia: This is an oil of self-assurance reminding you to live from your true self. It brings comfort to the heart. Use Cassia as a flavoring in cooking. It's similar in flavor to cinnamon, making it a nice addition to Indian dishes.

♡ Suns, Moons, and Success. Learn more: www.ChooseBigChange.com ♡

SEEKING PERFECTION: PRASARITA PADOTTANASANA (WIDE-LEGGED STANDING FORWARD BEND)

Prasarita: "spread out"; *pada:* "foot"; *uttan:* "extended"; *asana:* "pose"

It can be said that there are two kinds of people in this world: the seekers and the finders. There is a vast difference between seeking and finding. But for Virgos, the quest in life seems to always be in the joy of seeking the perfection of the profound. We can learn something from this by learning how to harness our own inner discernment and idealism and looking at ways we can reach higher, aim straighter, and keep seeking that perfection even after we think we have found what we were looking for.

Prasarita padottanasana, or Wide-Legged Standing Forward Bend, is a yoga pose to remind us that even when we think we have finished our search, there is still so much to learn. This pose is one that has many options to advance into once you master the initial beginner movement. Many practitioners use this pose as a starting point for headstands and arm balancing poses. There are a myriad of variations to Wide-Legged Standing Forward Bend that can be performed as well. Such a "simple" pose, yet so many ways to perfect and further it.

This pose is very helpful in easing anxiety and stress.

WIDE-LEGGED STANDING FORWARD BEND

1. Stand with your legs about one arms' length apart, straight and with your feet pointing forward. Extend your arms straight out to the sides, level with the floor. Think "ankle to wrist" with your wrist directly above your ankles.

2. Press into your heels and straighten your spine.

3. Turn your big toes in slightly to feel the outer edges of the feet.

4. Bring your hands to your hips and engage your abdomen. Inhale.

5. On the exhale, with a flat back and straight legs, bend forward from the waist as far as you comfortably can.

6. Inhale and bring your hands to the ground, fingers pointing forward. Don't be concerned if you can't reach the floor, just reach as far down as you can. Breathe here for a moment.

7. You can choose to reach your arms toward the back slightly to deepen the pose.

8. To go deeper still, you can choose to bring the crown of the head toward the ground. Breathe here for as long as you'd like. Eventually, you might want to lay the top of your head on the ground. Go slowly and perfect every movement before moving on to variations.

9. To come out of the pose, inhale and bring your hands back to your hips and lift your torso on the exhale. Bring feet back together in one step. Repeat if you wish, adding variations and perfecting the pose.

Chew on This

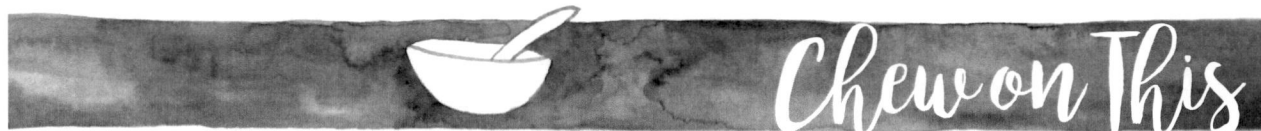

Did you know your gut is your second brain? Did you know that your gut is the gateway to disease, or "dis-ease"? Did you know that 90% of our serotonin (the chemical that makes us happy and feel good) is produced in the gut? All of these reasons are why gut health is all the buzz. Here are our top four tips for improving your gut and therefore the way you think and feel!

1. **Cleanse with clean water.** The quality of the water you're drinking is just as important as the quantity. Everything from agriculture to chemicals from industry runoff to household plumbing can affect the quality of tap water. Drinking spring or filtered water can help reduce your exposure to contaminants sometimes found in tap water. Use a good home filter to reduce exposure to common contaminants such as chromium, lead, and atrazine. As you're hydrating, don't forget to go green! Reusable stainless steel, glass, or BPA-free water bottles and home water filters support not only the health of your gut but also the health of the planet.

2. **Manage stress with meditation.** Because fast-paced lifestyles and high-stress environments have become the norm, we often don't realize their negative impact on our well-being. Using meditation to combat stress can help clear the mind, improve breathing, promote relaxation, and discourage disjointed coping strategies. Meditation is a go-to resource anytime and anyplace for a quick timeout to manage stress. Try a quick couple of breaths in the bathroom or in your car; no one is too busy to still the mind, even if just for a minute or two.

3. **Prebiotics & Probiotics.** Probiotics have been in the wellness spotlight for a while now, but prebiotics (a form of dietary fiber found in plant-based foods that promotes the growth of good bacteria) are equally important. Sources of prebiotics include flaxseeds, berries, garlic, onions, asparagus, watermelon, and grapefruit (to list a few). Both probiotics and pre-biotics improve digestion, mood, reduce inflammation, boost immunity, and so much more.

4. **Move your body to optimize gut health.** In addition to getting those endorphins flowing and keeping you in shape, moving can also increase blood flow and stimulate the bowels. Have you ever had to run to the bathroom during or after certain exercises? It is suggested that 30 minutes of movement five times a week will improve both your gut and overall health. In fact, physical activity can actually increase the diversity of bacteria in your gut, a sign of good gut health. Be intuitive as to how and when your body wants to move. For some, it's yoga, for others, it's high intensity training. Either way, the body is designed to move, to heal and nurture itself. So, get moving.

Health Hint

It is absolutely necessary to put your personal house, your energy body, in order. Your energy body takes precedence over your physical body. By adding energy exercises to your days, you will amplify your auric field, stimulate your brain, create proper flow for your meridians, and your physical body will have more balance. You may also provide yourself your own attitude adjustment as you notice the swift changes that happen. Start your new personal energy practice by doing the Four Thumps from The Eden Method. Use just your fingertips to thump or tap as follows.

- Thump under your eyes, 5-7 seconds.
- Thump your sternum, 5-7 seconds.
- Thump at the widest part of your clavicle, just below it, at the soft spots on both sides, 5-7 seconds.
- Thump at your first rib, just above the waist, both sides, 5-7 seconds.

♡ Suns, Moons, and Success. Learn more: www.ChooseBigChange.com ♡

Page 117

Notes

Grab your free bonuses here: www.ChooseBigChange.com/bonus21

✻ www.TheEnergyAlmanac.com ✻

October

MODERATION, PERSPECTIVE, RECONCILIATION

OCTOBER 4-10

Do decide what new direction you might take.
Do not go too far too fast.

OCTOBER 11-17

Do work to regain a positive perspective.
Do not push your point of view; go easy.

OCTOBER 18-24

Do focus on seeing all the pieces of the puzzle.
Do not ignore the warning signs.

OCTOBER 25-31

Do become aware of your need to control.
Do not fall prey to victimhood or martyrdom.

Laugh as much as you breathe

Love as long as you live.

WHAT IS THE BENEFIT OF FOCUS AND ACTION?

OCTOBER 6

NEW MOON IN 13° LIBRA

Maintaining Balance

OCTOBER 20

FULL MOON IN 27° ARIES

Harmonious Actions

♡ Suns, Moons, and Success. Learn more: www.ChooseBigChange.com ♡

Energy Almanac 2021 EDITION

Page 119

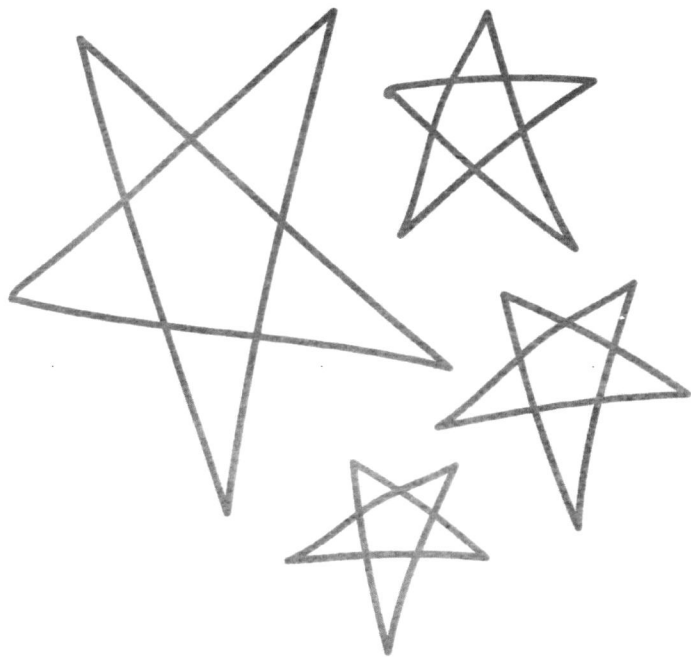

October

---◇◆◇---

Solar Cycle:
4TH QUARTER
Keywords:
MODERATION, PERSPECTIVE, RECONCILIATION

With Sun, Mercury, and Mars in Libra, emphasis remains on relationships, agreements, contracts, and legal matters. It takes work, but there is resolution in some of these Libra areas. However, just like this sign's symbol of the scales, the energy will shift. Notice the increased intensity. It will be a period for focus and action.

October brings a welcome return to direct motion for Pluto, Saturn, Jupiter, and Mercury, in that order. Though last to take place, Mercury's direct motion on the 18th at 11:17 a.m. EDT is first to have noticeable effects. In the dark phase of the solar year, new perceptions are welcome. It's the perfect time to reassess and develop strategies. These concepts will be applicable during the waxing solar cycle coming in early 2022. But the forward motion of those outer planets, especially Jupiter, will begin to open the flow for activity in other areas.

Venus moves into playful Sagittarius on the 7th which brightens up the area of relationships in general. In this expansive sign, Venus enjoys philosophy, learning about different cultures, and exploring beliefs. People may seem hard to pin down now. Notice they are frequently on the move.

When the Sun enters Scorpio on the 23rd, you can dive deeper into your feelings. Remember those who have passed on. Self-expression can have powerful effects. Put your focus on commitments, right use of shared resources, and financial areas of loans, insurance, income tax, and inheritance. There's added passion in those areas when Mars enters Scorpio on the 30th.

DATES TO WATCH:

- **October 1-2 Mercury square Pluto, Venus square Jupiter, Venus sextile Pluto.** A communication barrier carries over from September and overoptimism is in play. Approach carefully and with the guidance of a powerful pundit.

- **October 5-10 Sun conjunct Mars, Pluto resumes direct motion, Mercury conjunct Mars, Saturn resumes direct motion.** Watch for expressing opinions and pushing too hard in discussions.

- **October 6 New Moon in Libra.** *See October Moons section.*

- **October 13-15 Venus sextile Saturn, Sun trine Jupiter.** Expect green lights, wise advice, and a restoration of harmony in relationships.

- **October 18 Mercury and Jupiter turn direct.** Improved communication and much clearer thinking are available.

- **October 20 Full Moon in Aries.** *See October Moons section.*

- **October 21-23 Mars square Pluto.** Fighting for a point of view has serious consequences.

- **October 26-27 Venus square Neptune.** All smiles are not sincere, and all that glitters is not gold.

♡ Suns, Moons, and Success. Learn more: www.ChooseBigChange.com ♡

OCTOBER ASTROLOGY BY THE WEEKS

OCTOBER 4–10

Lunar Signs:
VIRGO, LIBRA, SCORPIO, SAGITTARIUS
Lunar Cycle:
4TH QUARTER, NEW, 1ST QUARTER

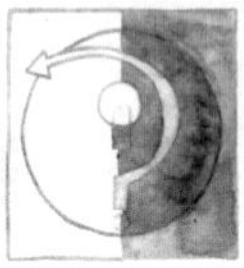
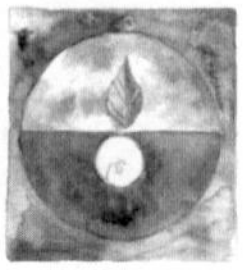

Mercury trine Jupiter brings good news. New Moon in Libra and Venus enters Sagittarius, shifting values and love nature. Sun conjunct Mars energizes self-expression. Sun conjunct Mercury and Mercury conjunct Mars indicates communications may exceed boundaries.

The planetary energies bring good news! You may sense a desire for a new start in a relationship or a more playful love nature. Notice, though, that everyone seems overeager to impress their viewpoints. Shore up your patience.

Your thoughts, communications, and negotiation abilities are highlighted this week. There can be good news and an old discussion may resurface about plans for the future. As the New Moon gets closer, use this to reveal places that need to be cleared or released for greater success. Decide what choices and new agreements you'd like to see take place in the weeks ahead. You feel more playful and ready for fun in your love life and other activities soon, but the way things heat up at week's end is not exactly what you had in mind. Try hard to stay balanced or reach a compromise if heated opinions are being exchanged. Having Mars' fiery energy involved in the areas of self-expression, thoughts, and communications can cause you and others to push too far too fast.

Shadow:
It's time to pump the brakes. Slow down and watch for too much acceleration. Take time to relax; there is no need to rush.

OCTOBER 11–17

Lunar Signs:
SAGITTARIUS, CAPRICORN, AQUARIUS, PISCES
Lunar Cycle:
1ST QUARTER, 2ND QUARTER

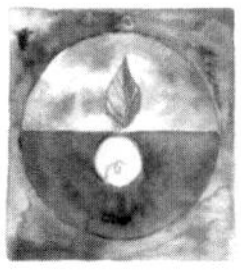
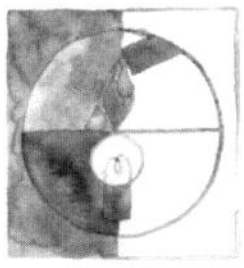

Venus conjunct South Node can overdo emotion. Venus sextile Saturn restores workable plans. Sun trine Jupiter gives us the appearance that the future looks rosy. Mercury sextile Venus and Sun square Pluto, playful words and an intense focus on tradition.

You may feel the need to get away from everything or just have a hissy fit. This is leftover energy from last week's disagreements. It's time to bring the scales back into balance. Cool down and regain a positive perspective. Remember that mentor from earlier this year? Wise advice is available to you and reveals the right direction to take for success. Inquire about relationships and the way to approach your goals. Communications are playful and you may hear what you want to hear now. But asking for partnership or a contractual agreement now could be stonewalled no matter how well you present your views.

Shadow:
Insisting on your point of view won't get you too far. Meditate on allowing others to be who they are while forgiving yourself and others for angry words and thoughts.

OCTOBER 18-24

Lunar Signs:
PISCES, ARIES, TAURUS, GEMINI
Lunar Cycle:
2ND QUARTER, FULL, 3RD QUARTER

Mars trines Jupiter at the Full Moon and successful actions accompany fruition. On Friday, Mars squares Pluto, bringing major conflicts to a head. Sun enters Scorpio on Saturday for increasing intensity in self-expression.

Go for the brass ring at the beginning of the week, but at week's end, don't push too hard for a contract or agreement from others. Control issues are on the rise.

You will feel uplifted and have good feelings from positive actions taken toward the future and in group activities. This is a time when all relationship matters come to a head; apply compromise. There is a red warning flag on Friday when any attempt to present different viewpoints will backfire, creating the potential for a major argument. Go deep when the Sun enters Scorpio. Here you can discover how a need to control and keep secrets (on your part or that of another) is interfering with the positive flow of communications in important relationships. Focus on seeing all pieces of the puzzle and you'll find better ways to manage things. There is a way to commit and share resources effectively.

Shadow:
Pay attention to warning signals. Don't be so quick to shift that you ignore what is right in front of you. Align with right timing.

OCTOBER 25-31

Lunar Signs:
GEMINI, CANCER, LEO, VIRGO
Lunar Cycle:
3RD QUARTER, 4TH QUARTER

After two quiet days, Venus squares Neptune on the 27th and sextiles Jupiter on the 28th. A friendly optimistic approach is open to idealization or deception, but benefits arrive and do include fun. On Saturday, Sun squares Saturn and Mars enters Scorpio, suggesting an unwanted obstacle could generate anger or revenge.

Uh oh. Warning, Will Robinson! Fantasizing isn't the answer to resolving last week's issues, and you could be wide open to deception. You may feel a temptation to idealize, see yourself as a victim or martyr, or simply escape into fantasy. All of those options are a negative detour. If it looks too good to be true, it probably is. Keep an eye on your wallet and check the bill for errors. Apply this idealized energy to your creative work and spiritual practice instead. This will bring expanded awareness of how personal energy affects future interactions. Open to receiving this gift and more good times with others as this week ends. Become aware of any need for control and these last days will go better. Resist attempts to achieve your desires "no matter what." Allow your strong feelings to be there and then practice the art of letting go.

As part of the last quarter lunar phase during the last quarter solar phase, spend some time in deep contemplation to receive visions for the end of the year and guidance about what needs to be released. You'll find what can be regenerated or transformed and brought with you into 2022. Spend the last day of October in harmonious discussions with those of like mind, and power will be amplified.

Shadow:
Fear and holding on too tightly complicates things. Loosen your grip on those you hold dear, including your ideas, projects, or partners. If they return to you, they're yours forever.

♡ Suns, Moons, and Success. Learn more: www.ChooseBigChange.com ♡

Energy Almanac 2021 Edition

All Rights Reserved Worldwide. Copyright Big Sky Publishing LLC 2021.

Page 123

October Moons

NEW MOON IN 13° LIBRA
OCTOBER 6, 2021 7:05 AM EDT

When the Libra New Moon arrives, you can set intentions for relationships, partnerships, contracts, agreements, and legal matters. The Sun and Moon join feisty, impatient Mars, while retrograde Mercury squares stationary Pluto.

Balance seems elusive. Communication, decision making, and gaining support may not be easily had. Come from a place of peaceful objectivity. Squelch the need to be in control of others, finances, or the future. Use your time stabilizing support and receiving creative visions. Consulting that trusted counselor can help you review your goals and it will be uplifting. It's time to gain insight about the right way forward.

FULL MOON IN 27° ARIES
OCTOBER 20, 2021 10:56 AM EDT

The Full Moon in Aries brings the need to reconcile the instinctive desire for action, individuality, and leadership against relationship, agreements, and harmony. At this Full Moon, the Sun (in Libra) is joined with Mars, firing up this usually peaceful sign and creating the potential for arguments, especially about what's right and fair. Relieve the tension by bringing more wisdom and love into thoughts and conversations. Once again, taking issues before your wise, objective counselor will help resolve conflicts.

Expect challenges from Saturn in Aquarius moving toward retrograde Uranus. This brings opportunities to learn more about how your personal energy vibration affects relationships and outcomes.

✶ www.TheEnergyAlmanac.com ✶

123 Numerology

A 6 month in a 5 year. As the crisp days of fall arrive, your senses may seek beauty, and your heart may be bursting to take actions that are nurturing and caregiving. You may catch yourself evaluating your intentions before you take action, thus ensuring you are moving forward in a way that is heart-centered and committed to the results of your actions. Be certain your heart is in the right place before making your move.

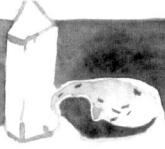

Gemstones

INDIAN AGATE

Indian Agate is a beautiful stone composed of many earth tones from green and brown to mauve. It activates both the heart and sacral chakras, inspiring healing and strength. With the sun, Mars, and Mercury in Libra and our focus on relationships, Indian Agate nourishes our heart center during this time and enhances our patience in all things. Receiving the calming energy of Indian Agate will be a great gift during times of conflict, frustration, and pushing too hard. This stone is magnificent for meditation. Create space for quiet to shift your focus away from doing and proving. Drop into receiving from the universe and the earth.

Keywords: COURAGE, PROTECTION, SERENITY, AND PATIENCE.
Mantra: MY PATIENCE GROWS WITH EACH BREATH.

Essential Oils

October could have us feeling unsettled as the energies ramp up and we step into action mode. This month there is a need for balance and moderation. Clarity will go a long way as will essential oils that stabilize your body, mind, and spirit.

FOR TOPICAL USE

Rose: The highest vibration oil to aid you in finding the balance you need. Dab a couple of drops over your heart.

Clary Sage: For clarity and perspective. Apply 2-3 drops to the third eye area. A gentle oil, there is no need to dilute or use carrier oil.

DIFFUSE THIS BLEND

- **Neroli 3 drops**
- **Frankincense 3 drops**
- **Lavender 3 drops**

Starting with the powerful stabilizing Neroli oil, add Frankincense for new perspective and Lavender for releasing tension and constriction. This blend of aromatics reveals a calmer you as it aids in addressing fear of being seen and heard.

INGESTIBLE OPTIONS

Green Mandarin: Green Mandarin invites you to find harmony and reminds you that there is always direct access to your potential. It can help bring you back to a lighter state of being. Take 1-2 drops in a veggie cap to help support healthy immune function.

♡ Suns, Moons, and Success. Learn more: www.ChooseBigChange.com ♡

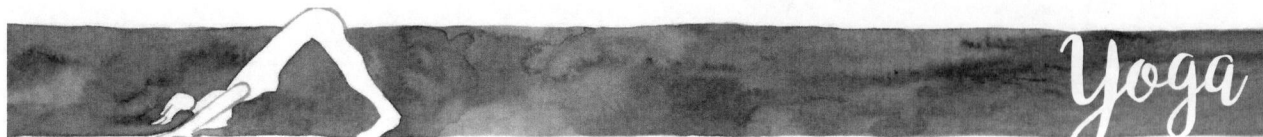

GOING WITHIN WITH PASCHIMOTTANASANA: THE SEATED FORWARD FOLD

paschima: "west"; *uttana:* "intense stretch"; *asana:* "pose"

Fall time for our ancestors meant preparing for the long winter months; the harvest was done before snowfall, grain was stored away, the animals sheltered, and preserves made. Once all the work was done, it was time to simply sit and be or find little tasks to do indoors. For us today in our modern time, we can use this time of autumn to do our own inner work of the mind, body, and soul connection. By focusing on forward folds in your yoga practice, you can utilize the power of reaching forward and within to find inner tranquility and peace through deep introspection.

Often in a yoga class, the instructor will use Seated Forward Fold as a signature of "now we start to wind down." It is typically used in class as the start of all seated poses. This month, we focus on Paschimottanasana in order to stretch ourselves out and within our bodies and our psyche. Where in your life have you avoided doing the inner work? Perhaps it has to do with finding the truth of your soul's purpose. Or maybe it has to do with digging up all the little things that you have been avoiding looking at in your life.

Seated Forward Fold stretches the back, hamstrings, and calves. It can be used alone in preparing for meditation or with other yoga asanas as a winding down point during your practice. While we work on perfecting and deepening Seated Forward Fold through the month, think of how you might improve your inner world.

SEATED FORWARD FOLD

1. Sit on the floor with your legs in front of you, stretched straight, feet together. You may use a folded blanket under you for extra support. Feel your sit-bones grounding you firmly onto the floor.

2. Draw your lower belly in and up.

3. Lengthen your spine on an inhale.

4. Fold forward, bending from the hips as you exhale. Reach your hands to your feet if you are able. If you find yourself rounding your back, lessen the fold. Bend only as deep as you can while maintaining a flat back. You may use a strap or towel to assist you in going deeper if you cannot reach your feet. Or you may rest your hands on your legs.

5. Keep all the length of your fold in your front body, paying close attention to your belly, ribcage, chest, and arms as they reach forward. Imagine a line of energy reaching from the crown of your head to over your feet.

6. With each breath you take, imagine going deeper into the pose. See if you can go further with each exhalation while keeping a straight back. Eventually, you will want to grab your big toes with your two "peace" fingers to really feel this more fully.

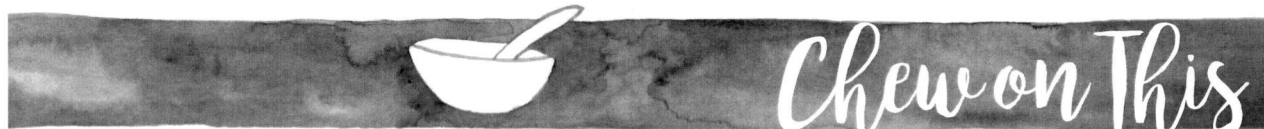

Chew on This

Sugar is in almost everything we eat today, from bread, cakes, cookies, and candy to canned vegetables, baby food, condiments, sauces, and "healthy" drinks and foods. Thanks to brilliant design and marketing, sugar gets labeled as corn syrup, dextrose, maltose, glucose, or fructose. Negative effects of too much sugar are weight gain, insomnia, ADD/ADHD-like symptoms (particularly in children), increased risk of heart related issues and type 2 diabetes, to name a few. This month's suggestion is to replace sugar with natural sweeteners like honey, maple syrup, or stevia.

Sugar qualifies as an addictive substance. Eating even a small amount is enough to make you want to come back for more. Quitting is difficult and causes withdrawal symptoms such as headaches, mood swings, cravings, and fatigue.

Here are five tips for dealing with sugar addiction:

1. **Reduce or eliminate caffeine. T**he highs and lows of caffeine include dehydration and blood sugar swings and may cause sugar cravings to become more frequent and intense.

2. **Eat foods such as sweet vegetables and fruit where sugar is naturally occurring.** The more you eat, the less you'll crave sugar.

3. **Get physically active.** Start with simple activities like walking or yoga. Being active helps balance blood sugar levels, boosts energy, and reduces tension, reducing or eliminating the need to self-medicate with sugar!

4. **Get more sleep, rest, and relaxation.** Simple carbohydrates, such as sugar, are the most readily usable forms of energy for an exhausted body and mind. If you are in a chronic state of stress and/or sleep deprivation, your body will crave the quickest form of energy there is, and you'll find yourself reaching for sugar.

5. **Eliminate fat-free or low-fat packaged snack foods.** These foods contain high quantities of sugar to compensate for lack of flavor and fat, which will send you on the roller coaster ride of sugar highs and lows.

Health Hint

Remember the Four Thumps from last month? Keep it up. This month, you can add The Eden Method Body Cross exercise to your routine. This will ensure your energy is signaling from left to right. The two hemispheres of your brain, the left and right, will communicate more easily, making eye-hand coordination and body movement smoother.

To do this simple exercise: Place your right hand at your left shoulder and drag it down and across your body to meet your right hip. Shake off your hand at the end of that stroke. Repeat two more times on that side. Reverse and use your left hand on the right shoulder and drag to your left hip, always shaking off the hand at the end of each movement. Repeat two more times.

♡ Suns, Moons, and Success. Learn more: www.ChooseBigChange.com ♡

Notes

◇◆◇

✿ www.TheEnergyAlmanac.com ✿

November

REFLECT, MANAGE, RECEIVE

NOVEMBER 1–7

Do expect a roller coaster of emotions.
Do not stay rigid in body or mind.

NOVEMBER 8–14

Do be willing to let go.
Do not refuse to compromise.

NOVEMBER 15–21

Do watch for overly emotional responses.
Do not overthink things.

NOVEMBER 22–28

Do notice the return of optimism.
Do not be righteous in your opinions.

NOVEMBER 29–30, DECEMBER 1–5

Do apply practicality.
Do not over-identify with your thoughts.

Let THE WATERS SETTLE
YOU'LL SEE THE
moon & stars
MIRRORED IN YOUR
OWN *Being*

WHAT GENERATIVE CONTRIBUTION IS BEING CREATED THAT I CAN'T YET SEE?

NOVEMBER 4

NEW MOON IN 12° SCORPIO

Clear the Clutter

NOVEMBER 19

FULL MOON LUNAR ECLIPSE IN 27° TAURUS

Transforming Values

Energy Almanac 2021 Edition

♡ Suns, Moons, and Success. Learn more: www.ChooseBigChange.com ♡

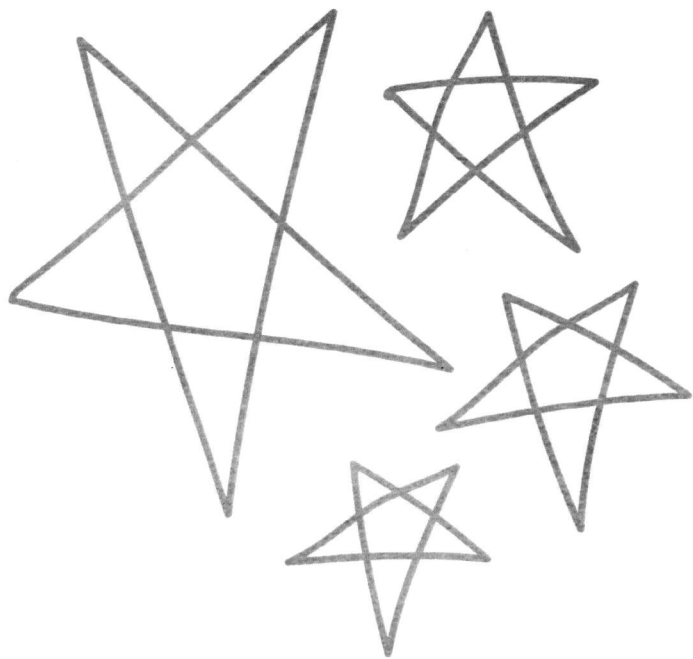

November

—◇◈◇—

Solar Cycle:
4TH QUARTER
Keywords:
REFLECT, MANAGE, RECEIVE

November begins with a Scorpio New Moon followed by sign changes for Mercury and Venus. Take the time now for reflection before choosing future goals.

Venus leaves Sagittarius for practical, earthy Capricorn in the early morning of the 5th. You'll notice a conservative, practical approach influencing expressions of love and personal values. Spending habits tend toward frugality, a trait which is also valued. Love of tradition leads us into the holiday season. Stay aware of a potential Scorpio pitfall. Mars in Scorpio engages conflict and discord from the 9th to the 12th as it squares Saturn in Aquarius. This provokes a contest between control and freedom. Mars in Scorpio opposite Uranus in Taurus from the 16th to 18th may find you or others roused to quick and possibly dangerous responses. This is in relation to surprising financial or material changes. In this deep-water sign, action is usually covert, creating unexpected, intense effects.

After this stressful period, the Sun enters Sagittarius on the 21st and Mercury follows on the 24th. Finally, the mood lightens! Notice that thinking shifts and conversation is more upbeat and humorous. Highly supportive aspects from November 18th to the 30th create an excellent time to take care of all mundane matters. Have enjoyable conversations. Receive creative inspiration and psychic input. Reach partnership agreements. This is what you've waited for! The 21st through the 29th brings positive energy to finance and romance.

DATES TO WATCH:

- **November 4 New Moon in Scorpio**. *See November Moons section.*

- **November 5 Sun opposition Uranus.** A surprising shift in worldly matters and values threatens control of assets.

- **November 9-13 Mercury conjunct Mars, Mars square Saturn, Mercury square Saturn.** Intense thoughts and passionate acts toward securing resources become frustrating.

- **November 16-18 Sun square Jupiter, Mars opposition Uranus.** Overoptimism and anger can take a violent turn.

- **November 19 Taurus Full Moon.** *See November Moons section.*

- **November 20 Venus sextile Mars.** This combination is good for relationships and creating workable structures in career and finance.

♡ Suns, Moons, and Success. Learn more: www.ChooseBigChange.com ♡

NOVEMBER ASTROLOGY BY THE WEEKS

NOVEMBER 1-7	**Lunar Signs:** VIRGO, LIBRA, SCORPIO, SAGITTARIUS, CAPRICORN **Lunar Cycle:** 4TH QUARTER, NEW, 1ST QUARTER

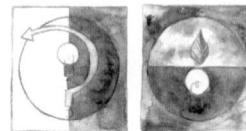

Mercury trine Jupiter and Mercury square Pluto stimulates optimism then obstacle. Scorpio New Moon and the Sun opposing Uranus means during your deep retreat you may be jolted by surprise. Venus enters Capricorn and Mercury enters Scorpio, making the focus for love and thought shift. Mercury sextile Venus brings accord and agreement.

This is a roller coaster week. In comes optimism closely followed by disagreement.

You may experience a disruption to your inner focus. Something is up in the everyday outer world and then comes a change of values complemented by a rewarding shift in thinking and communicating.

If you have meetings with friends or groups, expect positive, forward-thinking discussion and goodwill. Watch for a setback with someone set on maintaining the status quo.

You can set goals at the New Moon but be ready for a surprising upset and differences about finance, values, and who's in control. On Friday, use practical ways to discuss those issues and (hopefully) agreement can be reached by Saturday. You can enjoy the results and apply this positive energy to partnership, finance, and career matters for the rest of the weekend.

*If you haven't done so already, order The Energy Almanac for 2022. Go to www.TheEnergyAlmanac.com or amazon.com today.

Shadow:
Beware of overattachment. Release rigidity in body and mind. Be flexible and allow for new ideas and experiences to be present.

NOVEMBER 8-14	**Lunar Signs:** CAPRICORN, AQUARIUS, PISCES, ARIES **Lunar Cycle:** 1ST QUARTER, 2ND QUARTER

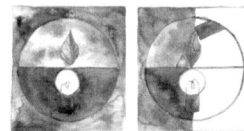

Mercury conjunct Mars, Mercury square Saturn, Mars square Saturn all add up to a day of red flags and frustration. Sun trine Neptune gives psychic insight. Mercury opposed Uranus throws a curve ball.

This week will remind you of January. Look for insight into the deeper meanings of issues and how to let go when holding on hurts.

After a deceptively calm beginning where you still feel the positive effects of the weekend, you may collide with a major conflict. Someone wants to control resources, but methods and timing of others is in the way. This may also point to conflicts in group affiliations or a circle of friends. This could affect future goals. There seems an unwillingness to shift. Beware of creating or receiving bruises on the physical, mental, and/or emotional levels.

On Friday, surrender to receiving inner guidance. It's likely that motivations, yours or others, will be revealed. Your best laid plans may be thrown off course as another surprise occurs on Saturday. It's also a time when a secret may be revealed.

Shadow:
Refusing to surrender or compromise is helpful to nobody. Allow others to be who they are while forgiving angry words and thoughts.

✳ www.TheEnergyAlmanac.com ✳

NOVEMBER 15-21

Lunar Signs:
ARIES, TAURUS, GEMINI, CANCER
Lunar Cycle:
2ND QUARTER, FULL, 3RD QUARTER

Sun square Jupiter brings up control issues. Sun sextile Pluto moves projects along. Mars opposes Uranus and creates a potential for volatile reactions, and Mercury trine Neptune may bring psychic input. Venus trine Uranus, Full Moon in Taurus brings help dealing with change as feelings peak. Mercury square Jupiter finds you overthinking while Mercury sextile Pluto puts the ducks back in a row.

You may feel like this week keeps you on your toes with an important aspect to respond to every day. A red flag warns you not to overreact to sudden changes in everyday affairs. Meanwhile, energy grows for the potent Taurus Full Moon.

Be sensitive to deep feelings that might override your objectivity. This awareness makes it easier to soften any defensive response to surprising changes. Once the moment passes you may find it easier to understand what happened and suddenly know how to deal with situations in a more inclusive way. Let someone help you. Allow the assistance of a conservative helper so that situations are repaired. Find ways to make changes work while the Taurus Full Moon reveals discrepancies in values and ways of dealing with money.

Boundaries are important but don't be too controlling. It could negatively affect dealings with friends or groups on Saturday. You and/or others may be overthinking. Sunday brings the thoughts and advice that can put sound systems in place for success.

Shadow:
Don't get carried away overthinking or creating futures that aren't real. Check in intuitively to align with right timing.

NOVEMBER 22-28

Lunar Signs:
CANCER, LEO, VIRGO
Lunar Cycle:
3RD QUARTER, 4TH QUARTER

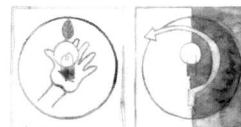

Sun enters Sagittarius, Sun conjunct South Node; Mercury enters Sagittarius, Mercury conjunct South Node. Spirits lift and optimism returns but don't overdo it Friday through Sunday a lack of planetary aspects allows time to enjoy the new energy while toning it down a bit.

It can feel good to be in the clear after shooting the rapids, but being overly exuberant is also an imbalance that can lead to unintentional alienation of others. Be mindful of righteous expression of beliefs and opinions. If you or someone else is in that state, notice the effect. Remember the desire to be right is in us all. Be willing to shift gears.

There are quiet days over the weekend. Enjoy the Sagittarian energy of good will and humor. It's a great time for an adventure to explore new places and activities.

If you haven't done so already, order The Energy Almanac for 2022. Go to www.TheEnergyAlmanac.com or amazon.com today.

Shadow:
Are you fully listening? This is a good week to practice truly hearing what others are saying and acknowledge them by responding with your attention. The art of listening can be a form of love.

♡ Suns, Moons, and Success. Learn more: www.ChooseBigChange.com ♡

Energy Almanac 2021 Edition

Page 133

NOVEMBER 29-30, DECEMBER 1-5

Lunar Signs:
LIBRA, SCORPIO, SAGITTARIUS, CAPRICORN
Lunar Cycle:
4TH QUARTER, NEW, 1ST QUARTER

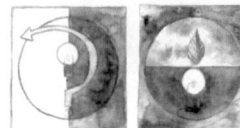

Sun conjunct Mercury, Mars trine Neptune brings identification with thoughts and aspirations to action. Mercury sextile Saturn, Venus sextile Neptune, Sun sextile Saturn on the 30th is thoughtful, helpful, and creative. New Moon Eclipse on December 4th is time to set intentions for the next six months in the outer world.

The last days of November bring uplifting, cooperative energy. Use these quiet days to review and assimilate events.

Though it may seem perfectly right, don't overidentify with what can turn out to be fleeting thoughts and perceptions. If you express them in a dramatic, dogmatic way, you may need to repent later. Use the positive and more grounded support coming in on a practical level. Let it blend creative visions with inspired conversations. Plan festive gatherings and share thoughts about future goals. Benefits come on the 30th from participating in activities with like-minded people with a similar vision for the future.

Allow time for dreaming and reflecting over the first days of December and look at previous events to see how your life may be changing during the first six months of 2022. All the signs are there. If you observe them well, you can create a powerful vision for the future and set it in motion with your intentions at the Sagittarius Solar Eclipse on Saturday. Consider home and work life, beliefs that need addressing, travel plans, and relationships. The Solar Eclipse heralds changes for the coming year.

Shadow:
Too much activity and not enough spiritual work makes Jane jittery. Align with positive spiritual tools that will help ground your visions physically, mentally, and emotionally.

November Moons

NEW MOON IN 12° SCORPIO
NOVEMBER 4, 2021 5:14 PM EDT

When the Scorpio New Moon arrives, set intentions for commitments, shared resources, loans, insurance, taxes, and inheritance. This New Moon near year's end holds the best energy for clearing away the clutter in your life on all levels. Stressful aspects to Sun and Moon from Uranus and Saturn may remind you of the energy of January. Seek a way to control the effects of sudden changes that have occurred and that may be ahead. Stay focused on securing structures for the future. Be mindful and focused on how your own energy affects and creates what's ahead.

Mars in early Scorpio, also square Saturn, suggests a need to overcome control issues that are born of fear and that which creates resistance in others. Apply good communications that blend insight with practicality to help ease current and coming tensions.

FULL MOON LUNAR ECLIPSE IN 27° TAURUS
NOVEMBER 19, 2021 3:57 AM EST

The Full Moon in Taurus brings the need to reconcile feelings focused on personal finance and values, possessions, and preserving, versus identifying with commitment, shared resources, transformation, and regeneration. Sun and Moon have vastly different ideas about how to deal with those areas, and fixed signs Taurus and Scorpio have a hard time letting go to resolve issues of compromise.

Get more information about finance and other concerns, preferably from that wise counselor. He or she can shed objective light on future potentials. This can also help relieve tension that may already be in place. There is loving, practical advice and some inspired, intuitive guidance to draw upon.

The last eclipse of the year, December 4th in Sagittarius, draws near. Events happening around this Taurus Full Moon can show you where and how some of the month's changes will manifest, so pay attention.

23 Numerology

A 7 month in a 5 year. This is a good month to start each day with "Who Am I?" In knowing yourself through introspection, you will advance. Slowing down is the best action for you now. Take a break from work and do things to address your inner landscape. Consider this month a well-deserved period of isolation and introspection.

♡ Suns, Moons, and Success. Learn more: www.ChooseBigChange.com ♡

Energy Almanac 2021 Edition

Page 135

Gemstones

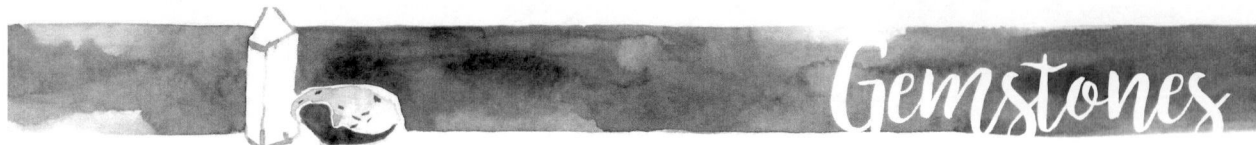

CRAZY LACE AGATE

Crazy Lace Agate is a charming stone of many colors. "Crazy lace" refers to the numerous bands and colors expressed in each stone which may include white, gray, brown, mustard yellow, orange, and rusty red. It activates the third eye and crown chakras, allowing greater access to vision and dreams. These energetic capacities will contribute greatly to the month of November. Amid conflict, upset, and obstacles, Crazy Lace Agate will encourage laughter. This lightness and joy brings you out of reaction and into the gift of the present moment. Carry this stone with you and meditate with it daily. Allow its subtle energies to calm you and balance the extremes of emotion. Release your suppressed feelings and thoughts and shift your focus to laughter and creation. Harnessing the earth element, Crazy Lace Agate supports releasing emotions and staying grounded.

Keywords: HAPPINESS, FOCUS, CONFIDENCE, AND LIVELINESS.
Mantra: I CLAIM, OWN, AND ACKNOWLEDGE THE LIGHTNESS OF MY BEING.

Essential Oils

There is a lot being asked of us this month. There is a call for us to release control and surrender negativity. As we do this, we are naturally placed in a state of reflection. You may find yourself uncomfortable at times. The oils can support you at this time. Allow them to lift you through the stressful periods and ground you as you move forward.

FOR TOPICAL USE

Douglas Fir: Apply 1-3 drops on the base of spine or on bottoms of feet. Douglas Fir teaches you to learn from and value others' experiences within family, especially your elders. There is valuable wisdom to be learned from the past if you'll allow it. Douglas Fir also aids in releasing negative thought patterns.

DIFFUSE THIS BLEND

- **Cilantro 3 drops**
- **Thyme 2 drops**
- **Cypress 3 drops**
- **Lemon 2 drops**

Energetic flow, releasing, and surrendering are felt in this powerful blend. There's a cleansing and detoxification happening for your mind, body, and spirit. Surrender to this beautiful combination and see what develops.

INGESTIBLE OPTIONS

Lemon: Lemon is a purifying oil that cleans out negativity. Add 1-2 drops to a beverage. Ramp up your autumn intake by adding Lemon to your tea with honey. In the morning, a cup of hot water with a couple of drops amplifies your AM routine. This oil can be used as a substitute for the real deal when you're cooking. Think rice, cake mixes, and salad dressings.

✧ www.TheEnergyAlmanac.com ✧

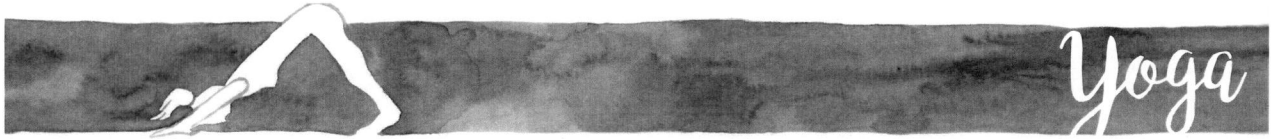

MATSYENDRA'S POSE & SPINAL TWISTS IN YOGA PRACTICE

Ardha Matsyendrasana: ardha: "half"; *Matsyendra:* one of the four founders of hatha yoga (whose name means "lord of the fishes"); *asana:* "pose"

As we start to turn in with the changing season, we tend to spend more time in sitting positions, often leading to back and shoulder pain. If you have a job that requires you to sit for long periods of time, such as at a desk and in front of the computer, then all the more reason to practice Spinal Twist yoga poses. This pose will release the pain and bring flexibility to your spine. With Thanksgiving and Christmas (and the coming winter season in general) also comes the potential for overindulging in food and drink. Adding spinal twists in your life will help aid in jump-starting your digestion.

In yoga, there is a whole cycle of sitting poses dedicated to spinal twists. Matsyendrasana is the best known of these spinal twist poses and is named after one of the founders of hatha yoga, Matsyendra (born in the 10th century CE). Each spinal twist has its own specific benefits, but the main benefits that all spinal twists share is to strengthen the back muscles, release pain, and stimulate the digestive system.

We will be learning about Ardha Matsyendrasana (Half Lord of The Fishes Pose) this month as a gentler twist variation of full Matsyendrasana.

SPINAL TWISTS

1. Sit on the floor with your legs stretched out in front of you. You may choose to support your buttocks with a folded blanket.
2. Bend your knees keeping your feet flat on the floor.
3. Slide your left foot under your right leg to the outside of your right hip keeping the outside edge of your left leg flat against the ground.
4. Step your right foot over your left leg, sole flat on the ground, placing it just to the side of your left hip. Your right knee should be pointing directly up at the ceiling.
5. As you exhale, twist toward the inside of your right thigh.
6. Press your right hand against the floor just behind your right hip and set your upper left arm on the outside of your right thigh near your knee.
7. Pull your front torso and inner right thigh tightly together.
8. Press the inner part of your right foot into the floor. Release your right hip area and lengthen your front torso.
9. Lean back slightly, feeling your upper torso against your shoulder blades.
10. Breathe and lengthen your spine as you twist deeper. Imagine that your spine is a towel full of water and you are twisting the water out of it.
11. If you wish, you can turn your head in the direction of the twist to go deeper.
12. Before releasing the pose and repeating on the other side, do a quick counter pose by twisting your torso in the other direction while keeping your legs in the same position.
13. Repeat pose on the other side.

♡ Suns, Moons, and Success. Learn more: www.ChooseBigChange.com ♡

Page 137

Chew on This

What really goes on my plate? How much do I really eat? Gone are the days where breads and pastas are your primary source of calories. We now know that a mixture of protein, carbohydrates, healthy fats and fiber make for a healthy human body recipe.

Here's what your plate should look like; be sure vegetables always take up the most space on your plate.

- Fruits may be fresh, canned, frozen, or dried, and may be whole, cut up, or pureed.

- Vegetables may be raw or cooked. Choose fresh, frozen, canned, or dried/dehydrated. Have them whole, cut up, roasted or mashed.

- Look for whole grains such as rice, oats, buckwheat, or quinoa.

- All foods made from meat, poultry, seafood, beans and peas, eggs, processed soy products, nuts, and seeds are considered part of the protein foods group.

- Choose healthy fats and oils such as avocado (whole and oil), olive (whole and oil), and nuts.

Remember, food goes far beyond our plate. Be sure you have a healthy daily dose of spirituality, physical activity, boundaries, and happiness in your life as well as in relationships and career.

Health Hint

If you're feeling anxious you can calm your subconscious mind by addressing your amygdala, the almond shaped nugget on both sides of your temple. The amygdala is your brain's emotional thermostat. To calm it, place your right hand under your left breast over the rib cage. Place your left hand just above your right arm's elbow joint. Hold this position for as long as you can, for up to 45 minutes. This position reroutes the nervous energy from the back of your brain and dumps it into the spleen which accesses all the blood of your body, thereby spreading out the anxiety and leveling it off. This exercise is from The Eden Method by Donna Eden.

Grab your free bonuses here: www.ChooseBigChange.com/bonus21

Notes

♡ Suns, Moons, and Success. Learn more: www.ChooseBigChange.com ♡

Page 139

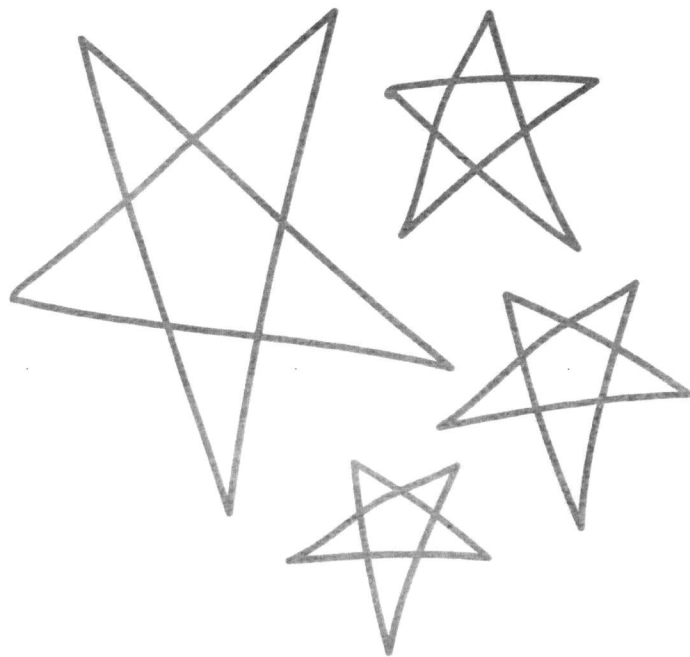

December

REFLECT, INSPIRE, ENVISION

DECEMBER 6-12

Do hold back on important decisions.
Do not project goals too far into the future.

DECEMBER 13-19

Do double check information before taking action.
Do not overdo or overreach.

DECEMBER 20-26

Do review your financial situation and what you value.
Do not skim the surface during reflection.

DECEMBER 27-31, JANUARY 1-2, 2022

Do focus on positive transformation.
Do not align with old negative patterns.

joy IS THE ROYAL GARMENT

WHAT INFINITE POSSIBILITIES ARE POSSIBLE NOW?

DECEMBER 4
NEW MOON SOLAR ECLIPSE 12° SAGITTARIUS
Passionate Protection

DECEMBER 18
FULL MOON 27° GEMINI
Seeding the Year Ahead

Energy Almanac 2021 EDITION

♡ Suns, Moons, and Success. Learn more: www.ChooseBigChange.com ♡

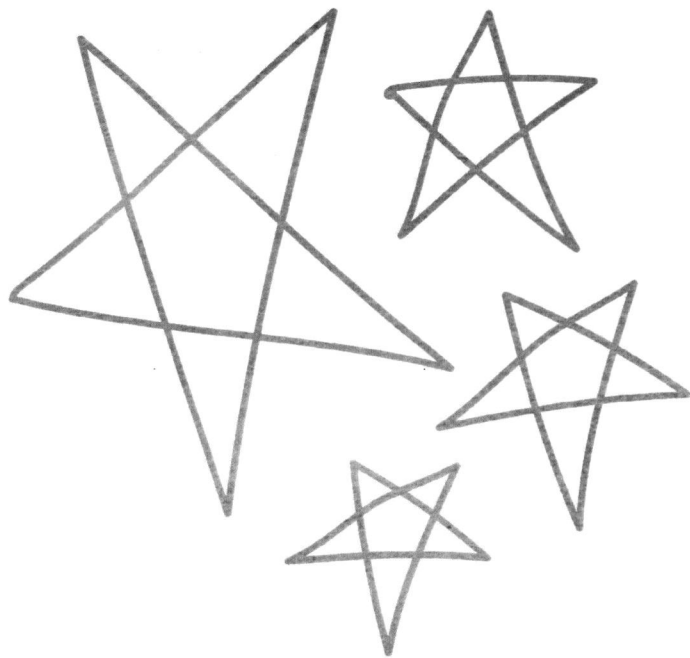

December

◇ ◇ ◇

Solar Cycle:
4TH QUARTER, 1ST QUARTER
Keywords:
REFLECT, INSPIRE, ENVISION

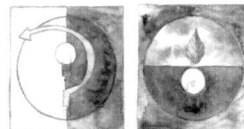

December brings seven major energy shifts to the end of 2021. Way to end the year with a bang!

Neptune direct brings inner visions, compassion, and spirituality to the world and also uncovers hidden deceptions. The Solar Eclipse at 12 Sagittarius foretells an end and a new beginning in your outer world of life within six months. These changes may affect the Sagittarius issues of beliefs, perceptions, philosophy, long journeys, inlaws, higher education, and those areas of the house where the eclipse takes place. (Check your natal chart. Book a reading as a gift to yourself.)

When Venus retrogrades in Capricorn, you can explore the deeper recesses and shadow self in relation to values and love. The focus is on traditions, status, career, family, and achievement.

The south node moving into Scorpio will give everyone an opportunity to look at the more negative qualities of this sign. This includes control issues, misuse of power, secrets, and other behaviors resulting from survival fear. You are asked to implement the higher aspects of this sign. Seek proper use of shared resources, commitment, positive administration and management, penetrating insight, healing, and using power for good. Apply the higher aspects of Taurus for forward movement: meditation, peace, grounding, connection to nature, right use of personal resources, care for the body, home, food, and healthy self-worth.

The Saturn Uranus square gives another opportunity to witness the exact moment of conflict between steady progress toward the future and surprising changes in the mundane world. We have had a year to explore this energy, and now we look at it with Venus retrograde, ruling the new North Node. There can be a different way of perceiving, experiencing, and acting; hopefully this brings peace instead of fear.

Like the sign of Pisces itself, Jupiter's shift to this mutable water sign holds the potential for expansion in both positive and negative directions. Positively, it brings expansion in spiritual awareness, compassion, philanthropy, and a sense of interconnectedness. It can benefit care for the waters and their creatures, and we may see prolific expression in the arts. Negatively, there can be expansion of drugs, addictions, and other forms of escapist behaviors.

The best way forward in December is to stay grounded in positive intentions each day. Focus on the future will help you navigate the shifting experience of the last month of 2021. Use the available energy to envision goals for the new year and set them in motion with intentions when the Capricorn New Moon arrives on January 2, 2022.

DATES TO WATCH:

- **December 4 Sagittarius New Moon Solar Eclipse.** *See December Moons section.*

- **December 9 Mars square Jupiter, Venus conjunct Pluto.** Pushing too hard for future goals.

- **December 11-12 Sun square Neptune, Mercury sextile Jupiter, Venus conjunct Pluto.** Destiny calls bearing gifts, but is all truly as it seems?

- **December 16 Venus conjunct Pluto, Venus retrogrades, Saturn square Uranus.** Love and power engage intensely. Matters of money loom large.

- **December 18 Full Moon in Gemini.** *See December Moons section.*

- **December 28-31 Mars sextile Saturn, Mercury sextile Neptune, Mercury conjunct Venus, Sun trine Uranus, Saturn Square Uranus.** Explore positivity and wisdom in action, inspired vision, and harmonious communications. Help may arrive from authority figures.

- **January 2, 2022 Capricorn New Moon.** This is the perfect opportunity to set intentions.

♡ Suns, Moons, and Success. Learn more: www.ChooseBigChange.com ♡

DECEMBER ASTROLOGY BY THE WEEKS

DECEMBER 6-12	**Lunar Signs:** CAPRICORN, AQUARIUS, PISCES, ARIES **Lunar Cycle:** 1ST QUARTER, 2ND QUARTER

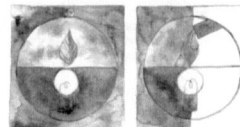

Mars sextile Pluto on Monday supports career goals, Mercury square Neptune on Tuesday brings confusion and deception. Mars square Jupiter puts energy in overdrive. Venus conjunct Pluto and Mercury sextile Jupiter brings powerful meetings and beneficial communications. Sun square Neptune causes questions.

After the downshift of energy of the Sagittarius New Moon Solar Eclipse last week, you'll have a desire to take action on Monday. Be aware that all may not be as it seems, but better times may come as the week goes on.

On Monday, a desire to feel in control spurs action to support your goals involving career, finance, and commitments. If meetings go well on Tuesday, don't be overly optimistic. There is information that isn't accurate or is confusing. Hold back on making important agreements now and don't let this fog spur even more action. You may make others feel a need to assert their own independence or challenge ideas about the future. Have a meeting with someone in power. It can end with good advice and good news about your hopes and dreams.

Be mindful that when your self-expression appears to be poorly received, you may doubt yourself. Spend time pondering and processing, knowing big shifts are due to arise at the beginning of next week. There can be problems with long distance journeys and communications, so double check information and conditions.

Shadow:
Overconfidence can create false positives. Stay grounded and seek accurate information or risk your hope crashing.

DECEMBER 13-19	**Lunar Signs:** ARIES, TAURUS, GEMINI, CANCER **Lunar Cycle:** 2ND QUARTER, FULL, 3RD QUARTER

Mars enters Sagittarius, Mercury enters Capricorn and passion and thought shift focus. Mars conjunct South Node accelerates righteousness. The Gemini Full Moon arrives and reveals discrepancies in beliefs, and Venus retrogrades in Capricorn.

You may become passionate about the truth early in the week as Mars enters Sagittarius. Mercury (your thoughts) in Capricorn (all business) has a more serious, cautious, and conservative approach to ideas and conversations. Outer world issues and maintaining traditions in holiday plans are topics of discussion. Don't be self-righteous now. It will not help you convince others, just as an overzealous attitude by others will surely irritate you. Hang on; the dust will settle.

Entertain new or different information during discussions this week or angry words will be exchanged. Use this kind of experience for greater understanding of differences between yourself and others. You'll notice this polarity is brought to a head at the Full Moon.

In this last week of the solar cycle, you could feel unwilling to compromise to sustain a relationship and bring it forward in the next year. Seek the advice of that trusted 2021 mentor and avoid making a major decision involving relationship or finance until early February when Venus will station direct.

Shadow:
Don't be overanxious. There is plenty going on and temperatures may rise internally even as temperatures drop outside. This is a good time to get a reading by your favorite astrologer or spiritual guide. See our astrologer, Shellie Enteen, whose bio is in the back of this book.

✯ www.TheEnergyAlmanac.com ✯

DECEMBER 20-26

Lunar Signs:
CANCER, LEO, VIRGO, LIBRA
Lunar Cycle:
3RD QUARTER

Sun sextile Jupiter and Mercury trine Uranus on Monday bring good luck and new ways of seeing things. Sun enters Capricorn and the Winter Solstice arrives on Tuesday. Shift to North Node in Taurus and South Node to Scorpio on Thursday, changing the collective evolutionary focus. Friday brings the last exact Saturn Pluto square of the year along with surprising shifts. Venus retrogrades to join Pluto again on Christmas day. Mercury sextiles Neptune, bestowing some workable insights.

As Venus' retrograde in Capricorn begins, you can enter a period of reflection on how cultural traditions, family opinion, career, reputation, and achievement, all Capricorn topics, affect your love nature and values (Venus topics). Venus rules money, so a slowdown and review in this area is a smart part of the Venus retrograde cycle. But this week starts with inspired ideas, real opportunities to be had, and gifts to receive.

Reflection on the past year and hopes for 2022 can lead to a powerful ritual of release and creation for the days surrounding the Winter Solstice. Be sure you acknowledge your growth and progress in many areas of life over the past year. Give yourself heartfelt gratitude and appreciation. If you see areas where you feel you've fallen short, look at the situation with intent to discover if you can do better in the future or if the situation is something to leave behind. The new nodal axis of South Node in Scorpio, North Node in Taurus brings the collective evolutionary focus to areas concerned with survival. Reflect on Mars' recent transit through Scorpio. Check your journal to see what you were dealing with to remind you of Scorpio issues of control, secrets, and fear of loss that creates a negative need to manipulate. We'll be dealing with these topics for the next 18 months or so.

North Node in Taurus asks us to employ the positive qualities of transformation, management, commitment, workable strategy, loyalty, and pursuit of healing. This will help you reach peaceful prosperity.

There is a threat felt in the realm of future goals, friendships, and group affiliations. Explore this for a more positive focus to handle whatever challenge arises.

Saturday brings powerful connections to others and the value of traditional expressions of the season. This may also resurrect old behavior, patterns, and strong attachments. Use the intense feelings this brings up to learn and grow. Spend some time alone on Sunday to tap into intuitive guidance and greater compassion. Gentle insights are available to help you see a new way forward.

*If you haven't done so already, order The Energy Almanac for 2022. Go to www.TheEnergyAlmanac.com or amazon.com today.

Shadow:
If skimming the surface is your normal, now isn't the time. A deep review and period of reflection will benefit your future.

♡ Suns, Moons, and Success. Learn more: www.ChooseBigChange.com ♡

DECEMBER 27–31
JANUARY 1–2, 2022

Lunar Signs:
LIBRA, SCORPIO, SAGITTARIUS, CAPRICORN
Lunar Cycle:
4TH QUARTER, NEW

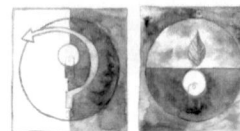

Jupiter squares the new nodes on Monday, showing evolutionary growth must include expanded consciousness. Jupiter re-enters Pisces to expand the realm of feelings while Mercury joins retrograde Venus, boosting our understanding. Mars sextiles Saturn, Mercury conjuncts Pluto to energize and structure thoughts of the future. The new year and the New Moon in Capricorn arrive on the weekend.

You will feel lifted by inspiration on Monday. Use expanded awareness of energy to create the highest good. The new influence of Jupiter in Pisces can be put to good use with spiritual practice and creative pursuits. Any conflict begins to be resolved and you find the combination of practical and loving words supportive in both friendships and groups.

Fuel your actions with truth and awareness and you'll be supported by those you've counted on for good advice this year. Deep thinking and past memories may bring a somber note to New Year's Eve, but keep your attention focused on anything that needs to change for greater success. This helps you feel confident when putting together a meaningful set of goals for the new year ahead. Instead of making resolutions you might break, use the Capricorn New Moon to set intentions after checking the 2022 Energy Almanac for advice on perfect timing in the year ahead. In this way, your goals are planned with support of energy trends. You'll find greater ease of accomplishment by being in harmony with the flow. Go get your next Energy Almanac now.

The last planetary aspects of the year hold a strong focus on spirituality, creativity, appreciation, and idealism combined with practical methods for future goals.

If you haven't done so already, order The Energy Almanac for 2022. Go to www.TheEnergyAlmanac.com or amazon.com today.

Shadow:
Don't focus on the past. Forgive mistakes and move on. Now is a great time to think about the year ahead. If possible, get an astrological reading for the new year.

December Moons

NEW MOON SOLAR ECLIPSE IN 12° SAGITTARIUS
DECEMBER 4, 2021 2:42 AM EDT

When the Sagittarius New Moon arrives, it is time to set intentions for beliefs, rituals, higher education, long journeys, inlaws, and learning about foreign cultures.

The Sun and Moon in Sagittarius between Mercury and asteroid Vesta bring alignment with beliefs and truth and with what you feel passionate about protecting. Seek to find balance between confused thinking and a structured plan for the future. Still in the shadow of Saturn square Uranus, you know the future can still hold surprising changes.

There is intense value placed on public life or a relationship that seems fated. Don't push too hard or overdo in that area. Draw on inspiration and you can find the way to balance these energies. Keep your eyes open for an ending and new beginning to occur in the house holding the eclipse. Check your natal chart to see where that is.

FULL MOON IN 27° GEMINI
DECEMBER 18, 2021 11:35 PM EST

The Full Moon in Gemini, the final Full Moon of 2021, brings dichotomy. There is curiosity, information gathering, logical thinking (Gemini traits), and identifying through belief, philosophy, truth, and seeing the big picture (Sag topics). The tension between Gemini and Sagittarius ideals are real. As always, a Full Moon is an opposition between Sun and Moon. The sun is currently in Sagittarius, the moon is in Gemini.

At this Full Moon, Sun and Moon are moving you away from confusion and toward optimism. You may continue exploring the qualities of both signs in this opposition, Gemini and Sagittarius. End this year with another consultation with your guide who can lead the way to a mutually agreeable middle ground. Mars trine Saturn suggests you'll take steady, beneficial action toward future goals while Mercury trines Uranus, providing you with practical thoughts about how to successfully deal with changes ahead. Do your spiritual work. It contributes to the exploration of values, love, and relationships, particularly in respect to the world you live in, tradition, family, and achievement. List what you're thankful for. It's time to reap the harvest of 2021 with gratitude and seed the year to come with positive visions.

NEW MOON IN 0° CAPRICORN
JANUARY 2

Read about this exciting New Moon in the area of business, big and small, structure, and discipline in the New 2022 Energy Almanac. Available at **www.TheEnergyAlmanac.com** or **amazon.com**.

'23 Numerology

An 8 month in a 5 year. This month will bring vibrations of manifestation, money management, and strength. The number 8 is one of divine connection as heaven and earth are symbolized by the two spheres connected vertically in a never-ending loop. What you desire (through Heaven) is grounded into earth. Manage yourself and your finances carefully, being flexible with what you have as well as with what comes in. Take actions that address the material world: balance the books, check schedule, review investments and check in on what you've been manifesting.

♡ Suns, Moons, and Success. Learn more: www.ChooseBigChange.com ♡

Gemstones

RAINBOW MOONSTONE

Rainbow Moonstone is an ethereal stone of blue-white iridescence. Moonstone has been treasured by humans for thousands of years and comes in many varieties: Peach, Gray, White, Cat's Eye, and Rainbow. You know as soon as you look at Moonstone that it explores hidden realms and mysteries. It activates both the third eye and crown chakras as well as cleansing the whole aura. With seven major shifts occurring this month, Moonstone really supports you on your inner journey. From cultivating inner guidance and knowing to enhancing happiness. Harnessing the wind element, Moonstone offers clarity on your journey. It is great for meditation, especially when exploring the inner realms of you.

Keywords: INTUITION, SELF-DISCOVERY, MYSTERY, AND DREAMS
Mantra: WITH EACH BREATH MY WISDOM AND SELF-KNOWLEDGE INCREASE.

Essential Oils

As the year comes to a close, we are asked to slow down, ground ourselves, and take this time to reflect and go inward. Connect with nature, your mind, body, and what we are putting in and on our bodies. Choose peace and love over fear. Reflect on this past year and envision what the future holds for you. The oils shared will aid you in renewing your faith in the future as they support both your physical and emotional bodies and open you up to what lies ahead.

FOR TOPICAL USE

Eucalyptus: Supports physical and emotional bodies. Apply 1-2 drops to your chest or throat. If you have sensitive skin use a carrier oil such as fractionated coconut oil or your other favorite.

DIFFUSE THIS BLEND

- **Black Spruce 4 drops**
- **Lavender 3 drops**
- **Wild Orange 2 drops**

Your mind and body will thank you as you drop Wild Orange into your diffuser and elevate to your highest and best potential. With Lavender you'll face your innermost thoughts and feelings and express them with ease as Black Spruce grounds you. This blend is perfect for spending your time in deep reflection.

INGESTIBLE OPTIONS

Wild Orange: This essential oil will elevate your connection to your soul. Take 1-2 drops under the tongue or in a beverage or bake a couple of drops into your favorite bread pudding recipe to boost the flavor.

SHAVASANA POSE
Śava: "corpse"; *Āsana:* "pose"

If you have ever been to a yoga class, particularly a challenging one, you know the pure joy and relief of going into Shavasana Pose. Even the name elicits a response: Shavasanahhhhh. But the pose is deceptive; while doing the pose, we must remain constantly aware, awake, and vigilant while also relaxed. At the end of any of my particularly difficult yoga classes, I always treat my students to a little stretch assistance while they lie in Shavasana. I might come around and pull lightly on their feet, stretching their legs. Or I might give their temples a little massage. And through it, I am talking; always talking. They might think that I am trying to soothe them and give them a little "treat". But what I am really doing is helping them to remain aware.

It's so easy for us to simply let go of our awareness in Shavasana; to let our minds wander and even to fall asleep. But the point of Shavasana is to let go of our bodies while keeping our minds in gentle awareness. We can master Shavasana by remaining in full awareness of our inner world, as if being in a state between being fully awake and fully asleep. By mastering this pose, we may come to even deeper realizations of ourselves.

SHAVASANA: CORPSE POSE

Lie on your back with your feet spread wide apart. If this hurts your back, you may bend your legs. Keep your arms natural at your sides on the floor, but slightly wide apart. Close your eyes. Be aware of your breath lifting and deflating your chest with your inhales and exhales. Scan your whole body for any tension and release it. Deepen your breath but keep your mind aware and open. Stay in this position for five to ten minutes. To release the pose, deepen your breath even more, flex your toes and fingers, reach your arms above your head, and stretch your whole body. On an exhale, bring your knees to your chest and roll to your right side in a fetal position, drawing the head in with the right arm. Push up into a seated position and gently open your eyes.

♡ Suns, Moons, and Success. Learn more: www.ChooseBigChange.com ♡

Page 149

Chew on This

It's super important to set yourself up for success. Creating your ideal life is essentially a combination of trusting your intuition and getting to know yourself (what works, what doesn't). These are the two best tools to use when looking to implement sustainable change. What works for you may not work for your partner or vice versa. Always listen to your gut and go with your instincts. Your gut is always right!

Life happens right? Here are three tips worth implementing:

1. Be prepared. For road trips, for busy people, or just because. Many times, lack of preparedness is the reason we reach for unhealthy food. Pick foods and snacks that travel well. Stock up on foods you like: nuts, trail mix, oranges, apples, bananas, and healthy protein bars. Leave snacks in your car, in a drawer in your desk at the office, in your locker at the gym. Choose grab and go items.

2. Fill up before you head out. This works well if you are going to a birthday party, work holiday party, or even if you're meeting friends out for dinner. In many of these scenarios we tend to graze and overeat, or we end up taking in something we don't want to. Being satiated before going out is key to making better choices in these group settings. It might seem counterintuitive at first, but you'll feel better later for doing it.

3. Keep it simple. What do I eat? Think whole foods. Foods that are still in their natural form: a potato, not a french fry; chicken breast, not a chicken nugget. Eat protein, fiber, fat, and carbohydrates. If you decorate your plate like we discussed last month, you'll be checking off every category. When in a pinch, prioritize protein for its ability to stimulate your metabolism.

Health Hint

Maximize brain function by using your entire brain; learn SuperBrain Yoga. Get your kids using this daily and notice the improvement in their schoolwork. Easy to do, this takes three minutes of your day. Start by taking your left hand and placing it on your right ear lobe. Be sure your thumb is on the top part of the lobe. Do the same with your right hand. Grab your left ear lobe with your thumb on top. You have just hooked your right brain to your left brain. Put your tongue to the roof of your mouth and draw in a breath as you squat. Release your breath as you return to a standing position. Do a total of 14 repetitions. Check out the many YouTube videos available for SuperBrain Yoga if you need a visual.

Notes

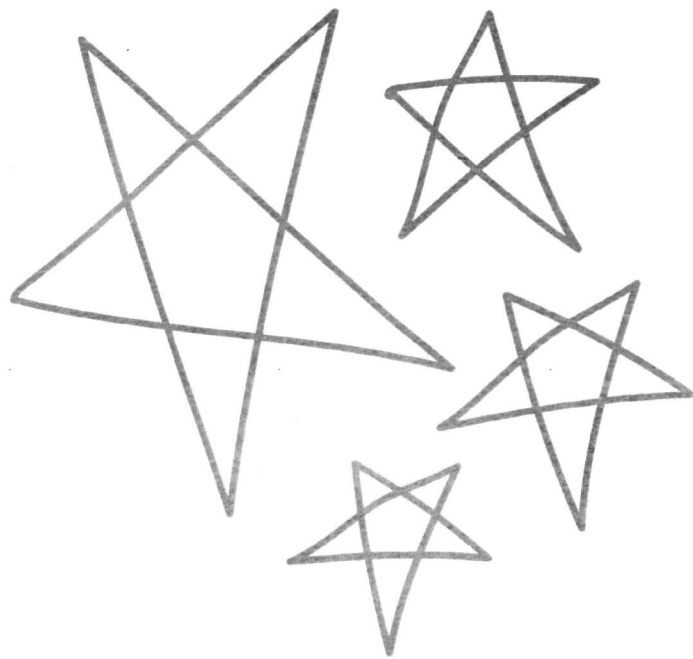

Coach, Publisher, Illustrator, Visionary and Voice by Tam Veilleux:

Tam Veilleux, SuperVirgo, is a quantum lifestyle coach and the proud owner of Big Sky Publishing and The Energy Almanac. Her passionate purpose is to help humanity connect the dots and evolve to their greatest version of themselves. Tam's goal is to make transformation fast, fun, and easy through her illustrated products and powerful transformational coaching services. You are invited to join her online or in-person astro-energetic retreats to help you be happier faster.

www.choosebigchange.com
IG: @Tamrav
FB: @TheTamraV

Astrology by Shellie Enteen:

Shellie Enteen has practiced astrology for over 40 years, combining Western, spiritual, and evolutionary astrology with knowledge of Bach flowers and aromatherapy. She has lectured for many private groups and has been a popular speaker at the South Florida Astrological Association and currently, Asheville Friends of Astrology. Her published works include "The Astrology of Bach Flower Remedies," 1999, The Mountain Astrologer, and Passion Planets, The Astrology of Relationships, 1980, Jove Books. Shellie also offers a mentorship program designed for individual student needs. Learn more and subscribe to the blog on her website and follow her daily forecasts on Facebook.

www.shellieenteen.com
FB: @Astralessence

Numerology by Dara Bailey:

Dara Bailey, Gemini, is a numerologist and spiritual advisor passionate about sharing her knowledge of sacred geometry and numerology. When she isn't searching for the truth in life, you'll find Dara stargazing for directions in the constellations and streaming soul code music by @Indi_Aura. Have your own personal numerology calculation or spiritual advising by Dara. Her partner company is www.divinetimingboutique.com.

consciouscreations888@gmail.com
IG: @iamdara1111

Gemstones by Kate Sarton:

Dreamer-Healer-Seeker-Observer-Creator Kate Sarton, Taurus, is a renaissance woman with a background that involves a variety of specialties all dealing with energies. A massage therapist, gemstone meditation bead creator, and energy facilitator, Kate Sarton adores being in the presence and space of possibility and is happy to help you create bliss amid the chaos of life.

katesarton.com
katesarton@gmail.com
IG: @kate.sarton.dunn

Essential Oils by Meegan Sciretto:

Meegan Sciretto, Sagittarius, is a holistic wellness guide and essential oil educator. Through her work she offers sacred guidance for the mind, body, and soul. Supporting women in reclaiming their health and radically up-leveling their well-being so they can live more full and vibrant lives is her work in this life.

www.meegansciretto.com
IG: @meegansciretto
FB: @meeganscirettocoach

♡ Love the Energy Almanac? Share on social media: #EnergyAlmanac ♡

Energy Almanac 2021 Edition

Page 153

Hatha Yoga by Kelly Cassidy:

Artist, astrologer, and yoga teacher, Kelly Smith Cassidy, Libra, has been deeply involved with yoga since she was a preteen. It is her intent to teach her students a holistic approach to yoga movement and its philosophy in order to feel for themselves a more comprehensive view of this ancient practice and way of life.

www.astrologysmith.com
IG: @CassidyAstrology
FB: @KellyAstrology

Chew On This/ Nutrition by Melissa Rivera:

Melissa Rivera graduated from the Institute for Integrative Nutrition where she learned innovative coaching methods, practical lifestyle management techniques, and over 100 dietary theories. Her education has equipped her with extensive cutting-edge knowledge in holistic nutrition, health coaching, and prevention of health issues. Her goal is to help clients more deeply understand food and lifestyle choices that work best for improving energy, balance, health, and happiness.

www.melissatrivera.com
IG: @melissatrivera
FB: @thetattooedhealthcoach

The Health Medium Hint by Ray Veilleux:

Ray Veilleux, Sagittarius, is The Health Medium. Ray has been doing intuitive health readings for more than a dozen years. He is well studied in everything from IET and Reiki to Qi Gong and The Eden Method. His depth of knowledge about the inner workings of the human body and how to amplify your health are well appreciated by clients across the world. Book your intuitive health reading.

www.theHealthMedium.com
FB: @TheHealthMedium

Editor, Susan Puiia:

Susan Puiia, Leo, is a comedy writer, editor, and writing coach. She's been writing sketch comedy and children's plays for community theater for over a decade. She believes everyone has a story to tell and takes great satisfaction in helping clients achieve their goals.

www.ninjaediting.com
Puiiaediting@gmail.com

Graphic Design and layout by Kendra Cagle of 5 Lakes Design:

Kendra received a Bachelor of Science in Graphic Design at The Art Institute of Fort Lauderdale in 2008. That same year she started her company, 5 Lakes Design. Her design and creative services range widely, and she has worked with clients from many different industries. She currently resides in upstate, NY, and works from her home office full time, while raising her two beautiful daughters, Lily, and Macy, with her husband Chris.

www.5LakesDesign.com
KendraCagle@5LakesDesign.com

⚹ www.shopBigSky.com ⚹